A COLLECTION OF CRIME COMICS

DARK HORSE BOOKS®

Editor **DIANA SCHUTZ** Associate Editor **DAVE MARSHALL** Assistant Editor **BRENDAN WRIGHT**
Digital Production **RYAN HILL** Book Design **JOSH ELLIOTT** Publisher **MIKE RICHARDSON**

Special thanks to **DEAN MOTTER**

Published by Dark Horse Books / a division of Dark Horse Comics, Inc., 10956 SE Main Street, Milwaukie, Oregon 97222

darkhorse.com

Library of Congress Cataloging-in-Publication Data

Noir : a collection of crime comics. -- 1st ed.
p. cm.
Includes bibliographical references and index.
1. Noir fiction--Comic books, strips, etc. 2. Crime--Comic books, strips, etc.
PN6726.N65 2009
741.5'3556--dc22

2009021290

First edition: October 2009
ISBN 978-1-59582-358-8

10 9 8 7 6 5 4 3 2 1

Printed in the United States of America

CONTENTS

"Crime is a fact of the human species, a fact of that species alone, but it is above all the secret aspect, impenetrable and hidden. Crime hides, and by far the most terrifying things are those which elude us."

—*Georges Bataille*

For Frank.

THE BOYS PUT ME IN A BOX.
OPEN THE GODDAMN BOX
by DAVID LAPHAM
THE BIG ONE'S NAME IS HUSSY, MIKE HUSSY, BUT EVERYBODY JUST CALLS HIM HUSS OR HUSSY.
HUSSY WANTS TO STICK VARIOUS THINGS IN MY BEHIND.
YOUR CLASSIC "RAPE ISN'T ABOUT SEX, IT'S ABOUT POWER" GUY.
AFTER, HE'LL PROBABLY SLIT MY THROAT.
THE OTHER ONE'S NAME IS KEVIN LEEDS. KEVIN SO BAD WANTS TO RAPE ME, TOO.
KEVIN, THOUGH, IS JUST A HORNY TEENAGER.
HE HATES MY GUTS, WHICH IS A BIG TURN-ON FOR TEENAGERS.

WE HAD AN INCIDENT IN THIRD GRADE.
HAPPY BIRTHDAY, SALLY!
SHHHHLIKK
JUST KID STUFF, REALLY.
KEVIN'S IN A QUANDARY.
HALF OF HIM KNOWS THAT THIS IS GOING TO END IN BLOOD.
THE OTHER HALF'S HAD A STIFFY FOR HOURS AND CAN'T WAIT FOR PSYCHO HUSSY TO GET THE PARTY STARTED.

MY NAME'S VIRGINIA APPLEJACK.
I'M GOING TO BE A WRITER ONE DAY.
THIS SHIT IS WRITER'S GOLD.
WHAT MAKES A SEVEN-YEAR-OLD ASSHOLE TURN INTO A FIFTEEN-YEAR-OLD RAPIST?
OR MURDERER?
WOULD KEVIN CROSS THAT LINE?
I HAVE A THEORY.
BOYS ARE PACK ANIMALS.
YEAH, THEY GET ALONG BETTER THAN GIRLS AT TIMES.
BUT THAT'S BECAUSE THEY'LL JUST BLINDLY FOLLOW WHOEVER HAS THE BIGGEST DICK.
METAPHORICAL DICK.
KEVIN HELD OUT THE FIRST NIGHT.
BUT WITH KEVIN'S MOM AND DAD COMING HOME THE NEXT DAY, IT WAS NOW OR NEVER.
WHICH WAS FINE BY ME BECAUSE, FRANKLY, I WAS GETTING BORED.

I MEAN IT, HUSS...I GOT A FIFTY-FOOT ROCK HARD-ON...
YOU'D BETTER NOT PUSSY OUT AGAIN.
OPEN THE BOX.
HEH.
OOGAH-BOOGAH!!
WAAH!
DUDE, YOU'RE PATHETIC.
HA, HA, HA...I ALWAYS KNEW YOU HAD THE HOTS FOR ME. SINCE THAT TIME IN THIRD GRADE.
YOU WISH, BITCH.
ALL THESE YEARS YOU WERE JUST TRYING TO MASK YOUR TRUE FEELINGS.
WAIT TILL I OPEN THAT BOX. I'LL SHOW YOU SOME TRUE FEELINGS!
IT'S OKAY. I KNOW BOYS ARE LIKE THAT.
BUT JUST FOR THE RECORD, I REALLY DO THINK YOU'RE A RETARD.

THE DAY I EVEN LIKE AN UGLY WELFARE SLUT LIKE YOU IS THE DAY--
KEVIN'S IN LOVE WITH ME. KEVIN'S IN LOVE WITH ME.♪
YOU'RE NOT EVEN A GIRL, YOU DISEASED BITCH...MUTANT... Y-YOU...
TEMPER...WOULDN'T WANT TO SHRIVEL UP YOUR GOOD TIME?
FUCK HER, HUSSY. JUST LET HER ROT IN THERE.
WHOA! HOLD UP. DID YOU...?
SHE'S RIGHT. YOU DID. YOU LOST IT.
ARE YOU REALLY IN LOVE WITH THIS GIRL?
I HATE HER GUTS! SHE FUCKING STABBED ME IN THIRD GRADE! I HAD TO QUIT BASEBALL! SHE--SHE--
THEN YOU HATE THAT BITCH, RIGHT?
YEAH!
YOU SAID SHE WAS POOR, RIGHT? NOT EVEN HER OWN MOTHER GIVES A FUCK ABOUT HER, RIGHT?
Y-YEAH... SURE...
SHE'S NOT GOING TO GO TO COLLEGE OR CURE CANCER OR SAVE THE WHALES.
SHE'S A TOTAL WASTE TO SOCIETY? RIGHT?
YEAH. RIGHT. YEAH.
THEN YOU OPEN THE GODDAMN BOX AND YOU FUCK HER.

AND YOU KEEP ON FUCKING HER UNTIL THROUGH ALL THE SCREAMS AND SOBS AND BEGGING...
...YOU HEAR THE UNMISTAKABLE SOUND OF A SINGLE, SOFT MOAN.
EVEN IF IT'S LESS THAN A SPLIT SECOND, SHE WON'T BE ABLE TO HIDE IT.
"THAT'S THE MOMENT WHEN SHE KNOWS SHE'S GETTING WHAT SHE DESERVES.
"SHE KNOWS SHE'S JUST A DIRTY WHORE.
"SHE LOVES YOU IN THAT MOMENT."
I--I DON'T KNOW, HUSS. SHE'S A SLUT--SHE'LL PROBABLY LIKE IT.
M-MAYBE WE SHOULD JUST TAKE SOME NAKED PICTURES TO--
NAH, NAH, DUDE. FUCK THAT. TOO LATE FOR THAT.
WE BANG THIS BITCH TILL DAWN, THEN SHOOT HER IN THE HEAD.
I MEAN, I THINK IF WE HAD PICTURES. Y'KNOW... SHE WOULDN'T...TALK...

YOU SEE WHERE THIS IS GOING, KEVIN.
OH, HE'S DOIN' IT.
HE'S HARD AS A ROCK FOR YOU, BABY.
OH...
...GOOD. THAT'LL MAKE IT EASIER TO FIND THEN.
I'M GOING TO CUT IT OFF WITH THIS KNIFE I HAD STASHED.
HUSS...
SHE'S JUST YANKIN' YOUR CHAIN.
HUSS, SHE'S CRAZY. SH-SHE MIGHT HAVE...
DUDE...
...YOU FUCKING LOST IT AGAIN?

ALL RIGHT...
KOK
UNGH!
HU--HUUU...
YOU BURN ME, MAN. BURN ME...DAMN...
CHK-CLIK
LOOK!
THERE'S NO KNIFE! SHE'S FUCKING TIED UP!

COUGH
RIGHT NOW, THERE'S ONLY ONE WHORE IN THE ROOM, AND IT'S YOU.
THE GOOD NEWS IS THAT I'M HERE TO SHOW YOU HOW TO BE A MAN.
GNNN!
THE BAD NEWS IS THERE'S GONNA HAVE TO BE SOME TOUGH LOVE.
NNN
NO... PLEASE...
THIS WORKS THE SAME WAY. WE KEEP GOING UNTIL YOU GET IT.
I GET IT! I GET IT!
I'LL KNOW WHEN YOU GET IT.

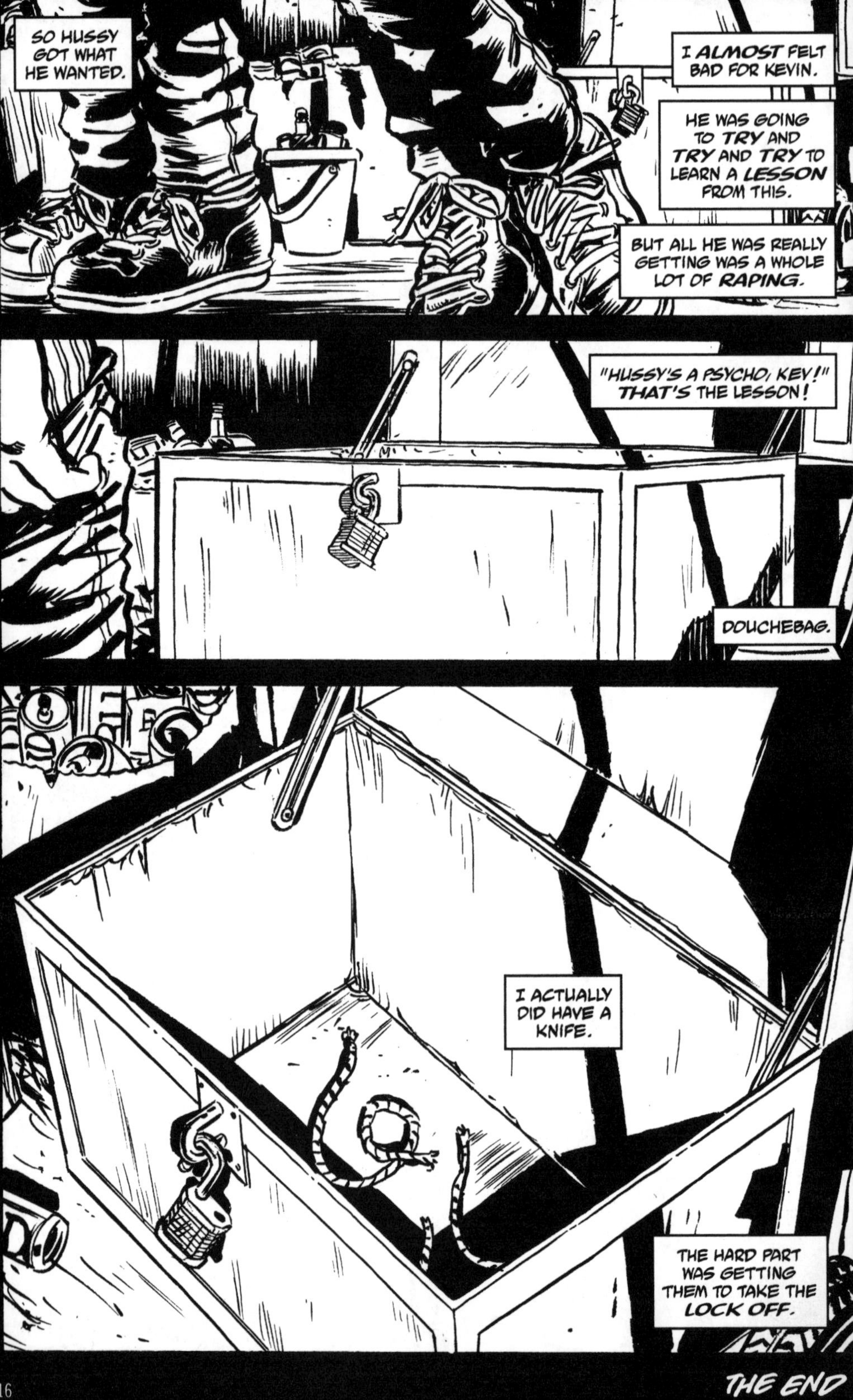
SO HUSSY GOT WHAT HE WANTED.
I ALMOST FELT BAD FOR KEVIN.
HE WAS GOING TO TRY AND TRY AND TRY TO LEARN A LESSON FROM THIS.
BUT ALL HE WAS REALLY GETTING WAS A WHOLE LOT OF RAPING.
"HUSSY'S A PSYCHO, KEV!" THAT'S THE LESSON!
DOUCHEBAG.
I ACTUALLY DID HAVE A KNIFE.
THE HARD PART WAS GETTING THEM TO TAKE THE LOCK OFF.
THE END

THE OLD SILO

PELTIER

DAMN!
SNAP!

GODDAMN PIECE OF SHIT.

HAVING TROUBLE, HENRY?
EH?

MR. LESSARD. CAN I HELP YOU?

WELL, HENRY, I'M AFRAID I'M HERE WITH BAD NEWS. YOU SEE, YOUR MONTHLY PAYMENT IS LATE AGAIN.

MARTHA?

I'M HOME, DEAR.

HELLO, DEAR. BEAUTIFUL SUNSET TONIGHT, EH?

LET'S GET YOU UP TO BED.

THERE YOU GO.

YOU SLEEP TIGHT, DEAR. I'LL BE UP SOON. JUST GONNA READ THE PAPER AND CLEAN UP A BIT.

LOVE YOU...

GAZETTE
BANK HIEST

SHIT.

GAZETTE
BANK HEIST

N W E S

N W E S

N W E S

N W E S

DEAR LORD!

PLEASE...

YOU GOTTA HELP ME. IT HURTS SO BAD.

YOU...YOU'RE ONE A THEM BANK ROBBERS FROM THE PAPER, AREN'T YA?!

PLEASE, MISTER...I DIDN'T MEAN TO HURT NO ONE...IT JUST ALL WENT BAD ...COPPER TAGGED ME IN THE BELLY.

DITCHED MY CAR DOWN THE CREEK, NEEDED SOMEWHERE TO HIDE OUT... BUT I THINK IT'S BAD...I NEED YOU TO HELP ME.

I NEED YOU TO FIX ME UP...CAN'T GO TO NO HOSPITAL.

I GOT MONEY, I CAN PAY YOU...

IT'S...

IT'S GONNA BE OKAY.

EVERYTHING'S GONNA BE JUST FINE.

JUST HOLD ON, SON.
OH, GOD BLESS YOU, MISTER.

MARTHA?

I'M HOME, DEAR.

MARTHA, I...

I KNOW THINGS HAVE BEEN HARD AROUND HERE LATELY...I KNOW I HAVEN'T BEEN MYSELF...

BUT, WELL...I THINK EVERYTHING IS GOING TO BE OKAY NOW. I LOVE YOU, DEAR.

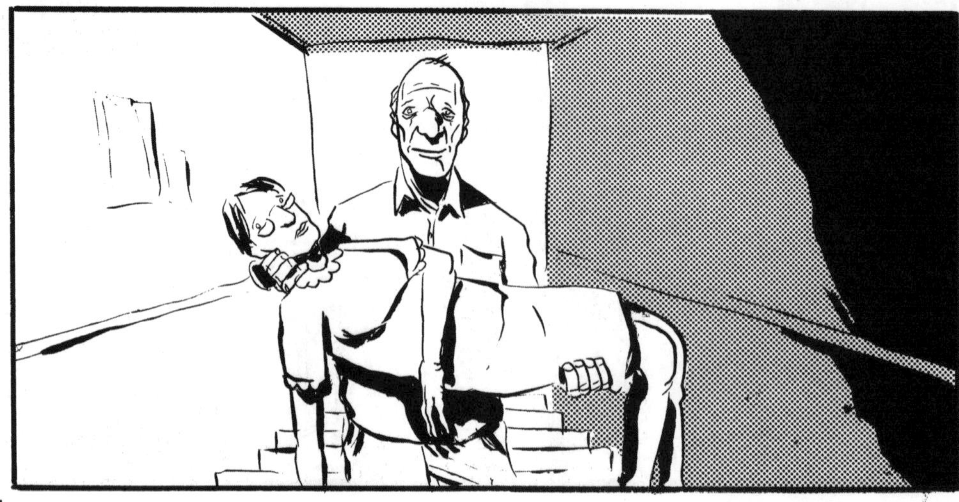

HENRY!
...MR. LESSARD.

LOOK, HENRY, I JUST WANTED TO STOP BY AND THANK YOU PERSONALLY FOR CATCHING UP ON YOUR PAYMENTS. IT WAS...UNEXPECTED.

WELL, ISN'T THAT KIND OF YOU. NOW, IF YOU DON'T MIND, I'LL THANK YOU TO GET THE HELL OFF MY LAND. I'VE **WORK** TO DO.

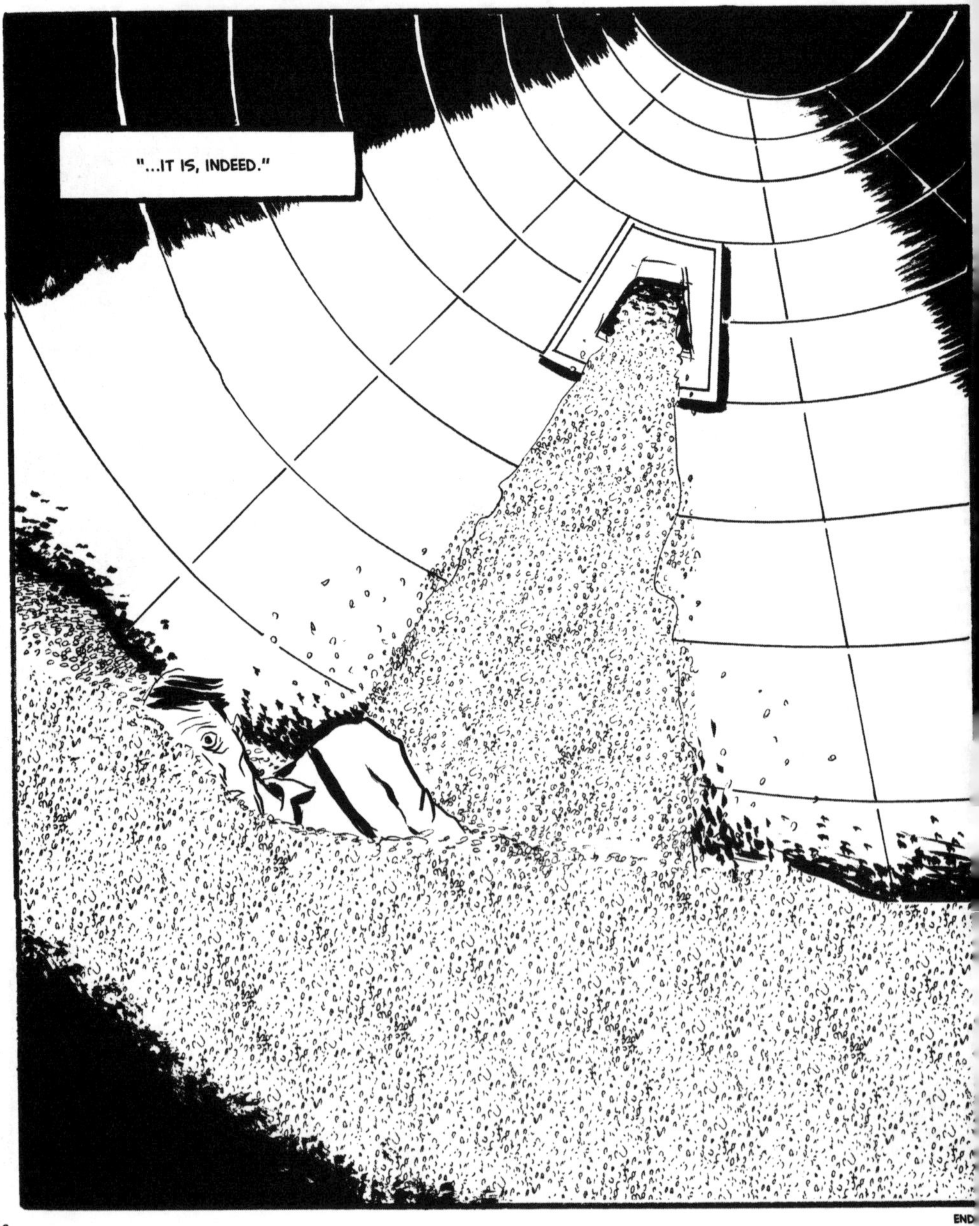

"...IT IS, INDEED."

END

ACHERON

MISTER X

BY DEAN MOTTER

THEY CALLED IT THE ANCIENT MARINER MASSACRE.

A PARTICULARLY GRUESOME INCIDENT IN THE DAYS BEFORE THE MALIGNANT EPIDEMIC OF SLEEPWALKERS, NARCOLEPTICS, AND INSOMNIACS HAD EARNED RADIANT CITY THE EPITHET SOMNOPOLIS.

YACHT ON THE STYX

AN UNSOLVED MYSTERY...

... UNTIL TONIGHT.

EARLIER THIS EVENING...
ANOTHER TOM EDISON?

YEAH. GO EASY ON THE VOLTAGE THIS TIME, GUS.

SO, HOW'S THE EXPOSÉ RACKET THESE DAYS, ROSEY?

CHARON
NEARLY EVERYONE REMEMBERS THE CHARON BUILDING, ONE OF THE OLDEST SKYSCRAPERS IN RADIANT CITY.

WITH THE COLLAPSE OF THE CHARON EMPIRE, THE CITY'S RENOVATION PROGRAM CALLED FOR ITS REMOVAL. WHEN THE DEMOLITION BEGAN, A STIFF WAS DISCOVERED IN THE CORNERSTONE.

WRECKING CO.

ANOTHER BRICK WALL, SINCE YOU ASK.

THIS WASN'T UNUSUAL-- IN THE CITY'S INFANCY, MOBSTERS, STOOLIES, AND CHEATERS HAD ROUTINELY BEEN DISPOSED OF IN LIKE MANNER.

THESE MORTAL REMAINS BELONGED TO SHIPPING MAGNATE VIRGIL CHARON, THE OWNER AND PRINCIPAL OCCUPANT OF THE BUILDING.

HE'D DISAPPEARED TWENTY-FIVE YEARS AGO, THE NIGHT OF THE MASSACRE, WHEN A GAGGLE OF PARTYGOERS ABOARD HIS YACHT WERE MYSTERIOUSLY SLAUGHTERED.

THE COLERIDGE DRIFTED BACK INTO HARBOR AFTER THE EVENING'S "PLEASURE" CRUISE.
BUT CHARON WASN'T ABOARD.

THE YACHT WAS SEALED AND HAS BEEN MOORED IN THE ACHERON SHIPYARD EVER SINCE.
I'M SURE THE STORY IS STILL ON THAT BOAT...

...LOCKED UP BEHIND THE SECURITY FENCE FROM HELL.
I CAN GET YOU ABOARD, MISS STONE.

YOU'LL NEED AN OVERCOAT.

SO, HOW COULD CHARON'S BODY END UP SEALED IN THE CORNERSTONE OF A BUILDING THAT HE HIMSELF CHRISTENED?

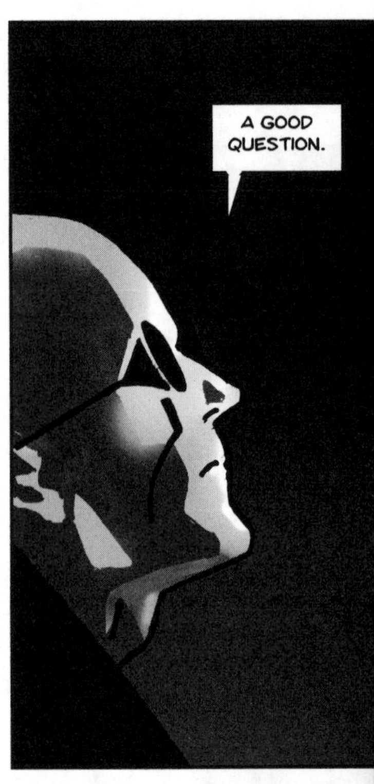
A GOOD QUESTION.

AND WHAT IS IT ABOUT THAT BUILDING, ANYWAY?
I COULDN'T FIND ANY ENGINEERING RECORDS. NO MUNICIPAL DOCUMENTS.

IT WAS A PRIVATE FOLLY, BUILT BY PLEBIAN CONTRACTORS. AN EYESORE.
THAT'S NOT MUCH OF EXPLANATION
I DON'T SUPPOSE YOU'D CARE TO EXPLAIN YOUR SECRET ENTRANCE TO THE SHIPYARD, EITHER...

NO LIFEBOATS. SO THAT PART OF THE STORY IS TRUE...
"WE"?
JETTISONED JUST AFTER WE LEFT PORT THAT NIGHT, SO NO ONE WOULD ESCAPE.

I WAS ABOARD.

THAT MAKES YOU AN EYEWITNESS. WHY SO SILENT ALL THIS TIME?

I'VE BEEN... BUSY.
PLAY RECORD
CLICK

THIS DAVIT HOUSED THE LIFEBOAT CHARON HELD BACK FOR HIMSELF.
SO... WHAT TURNED THE CITY'S MOST ECCENTRIC INDUSTRIALIST INTO A HOMICIDAL MANIAC?
YOU ASSUME HE WAS THE MURDERER.
THAT'S MERELY HOW IT APPEARS ON THE SURFACE.
12
14

ARE YOU SAYING HE WAS THE TARGET?
HE HAD ENEMIES. SERIOUS ENEMIES.
--WELL, COMPETITORS. RIVALS, SURELY. BUT KILLERS?
YOU'RE NOT THAT NAÏVE, MISS STONE.
YOU STILL HAVEN'T TOLD ME ANYTHING. WHAT DID YOU SEE?

WHAT DO YOU SEE?
THERE'S SOMETHING SINISTER ABOUT THESE OLD PICTURES OF CHARON.

"SINISTER." APTLY PUT. RIGHT-HANDED AT THE GROUND BREAKING --

-- BUT SOUTHPAW AT THE RIBBON CUTTING? SURELY YOU KNOW HE WASN'T AMBIDEXTROUS.

HIS WATCH WAS ON THE LEFT WRIST -- HE WAS RIGHT-HANDED...

STRAIGHT FROM THE R.U.R.* FOUNDRY.
SO MUCH TO DO AND SO LITTLE TIME.
HE DIDN'T HAVE THE CONSTITUTION FOR HYPER-DRUGS LIKE **INSOMNALIN**, SO HE SIMPLY HAD HIMSELF DUPLICATED.
RUR
BUT THE THING MALFUNCTIONED AND ACCIDENTALLY KILLED HIM. THE BODY WAS DISPOSED OF IN THE CORNERSTONE, AND THE AUTOMATON WAS KEPT AS A FRONT WHILE THE BOARD QUIBBLED OVER WHAT TO DO.

IN ADDITION TO THE LEFT-HANDED BIAS, THOSE EARLY MODELS REQUIRE CONSTANT TINKERING, LIKE EUROPEAN SPORTS CARS. OTHERWISE THEY GO **BERSERK**.

THE DOPPLEGANDROID WAS A TICKING TIME BOMB. IT BECAME CONVINCED THAT MANAGEMENT INTENDED TO DISMANTLE IT. THEY WERE THE GUESTS ON THE YACHT THAT NIGHT.

PHLOOM!

MY GOD! WHAT WAS THAT?!

OF COURSE...

*** R.U.R.**: ROSSUM'S UNIVERSAL ROBOTS-- OR "THE GOLEMWERKS," AS IT IS LESS THAN AFFECTIONATELY KNOWN-- THE WORLD'S LARGEST MANUFACTURER OF MECHANICAL MEN, BOTH PROLETARIAT AND BOURGEOIS.

QUICKLY!

THE MISSING LIFEBOAT WAS A DECOY, WASN'T IT?

HE NEVER LEFT THE SHIP... ALL THIS TIME... WAITING TO ELIMINATE THE LAST WITNESS, PERHAPS?

YOU NEVER TOLD ME WHY YOU WERE ABOARD THE COLERIDGE THAT NIGHT...
NO, I DIDN'T, DID I?
END

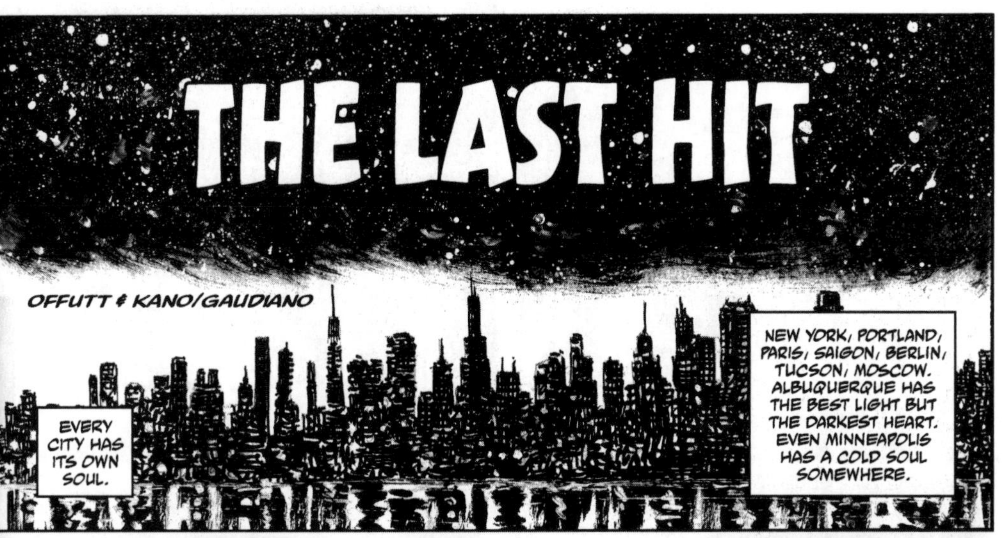
THE LAST HIT
OFFUTT & KANO/GAUDIANO
EVERY CITY HAS ITS OWN SOUL.
NEW YORK, PORTLAND, PARIS, SAIGON, BERLIN, TUCSON, MOSCOW. ALBUQUERQUE HAS THE BEST LIGHT BUT THE DARKEST HEART. EVEN MINNEAPOLIS HAS A COLD SOUL SOMEWHERE.

I'VE WORKED THEM ALL.
CRISTIES

THE SOUL INFLUENCES THE PEOPLE AND THE PACE, THE WEATHER AND THE TRAFFIC. IT'S THE HUM THAT CRAWLS INSIDE YOUR BONES.

EVERY CITY HAS A SOUL.

BUT NOT THIS ONE. NOT *SLATE*.

NO ACTIVITY. NO CHANGE IN LIGHT. NO ONE HAS ENTERED THAT ROOM IN A MONTH.

THIS IS MY LAST JOB. I SAID THE SAME ABOUT THE LAST ONE, BUT THIS TIME I MEAN IT. I'M LEAVING SLATE.

BUT SOMETHING ABOUT THIS JOB STUNK WORSE THAN THE HOTEL.
WHATEVER YOU WANT, HONEY. GREEK. FRENCH. HALF-AND-HALF. BONDAGE IS EXTRA. NO COMING ON MY FACE.

ANOTHER DAMN JUNKIE.
ANOTHER OLD DRUNK.

IT WAS THE FIRST TIME IN THIRTY YEARS MR. MACHINE HAD TOLD ME TO CALL IN BEFORE A HIT WAS COMPLETE.

AND HIS NEXT INSTRUCTION WAS **WAY** OUT OF LINE.
FIND OUT WHO IT'S RENTED TO. CHECK OUT THE ROOM. MAYBE HE GETS IN SOME **OTHER** WAY. COULD BE HE'S GOT A **SUITE**.

MY PERSONAL RADAR WAS PINGING LIKE A SUBMARINE.
PAID THREE MONTHS IN ADVANCE AND I AIN'T SEEN HIM SINCE. HE MIGHT HAVE **DIED** IN THERE AND NOBODY KNOWS. WE DON'T PROVIDE MAID SERVICE; EXCEPT THE KIND YOU PAY UP FRONT. YOU WANT TO LOOK FOR **YOURSELF**, GO AHEAD.

HERE'S A **BENJAMIN**. ENOUGH FOR **TWO** OF THEM SKANKY-ASS MAIDS TO HAUL YOUR ASHES. YOU DIDN'T **SEE** ME-- GOT IT?
11

YOU THE **INVISIBLE MAN**.
THAT'S **TWICE** I WAS TOLD TO ENTER THE ROOM. I DON'T BELIEVE IN **COINCIDENCE**.
IF YOU SQUAWK, **YOU'LL** BE INVISIBLE **FOREVER**.

ONLY TWO WINDOWS HAD A GOOD VIEW INTO THE **TARGET'S** ROOM. MINE AND THE ROOM ABOVE IT.
AND THE FUNNY THING IS, THE ROOM ABOVE ME IS THE ONE I'D **WANTED**. THE ANGLE WAS BETTER.

ROOM ELEVEN-- RIGHT, BOSS?
YOU GET THE DOUGH WHEN YOU COME BACK.
I PROMISED HIM TWENTY BUCKS TO ENTER THE ROOM UPSTAIRS.

THE SORRY OLD FUCK COULDN'T COUNT HIS BALLS TWICE AND COME UP WITH THE SAME NUMBER.

BUT HE'D GO UP THREE FLOORS FOR A BOTTLE OF REDEYE.

BANG!
AT LEAST HE DIED WITH HOPE.

LESSON ONE: NEVER GO OUT THE FRONT.

LESSON TWO: ESCAPE TO A CROWD.

LESSON THREE: NEVER STOP TO MAKE A CALL.

LESSON FOUR: DON'T FUCK WITH ME.

YOU WERE TOLD TO ELIMINATE THE FIRST PERSON WHO ENTERED THE ROOM. IT WAS A WET AUDITION FOR MR. MACHINE.
HOW'D YOU KNOW?

I WAS IN THE ROOM UNDER YOURS, WITH THE SAME MISSION.
I'VE BEEN AT THIS THIRTY YEARS. I KNOW WHERE THE BODIES ARE, BUT MORE IMPORTANTLY-- WHERE THEY AREN'T. THAT MAKES MR. MACHINE NERVOUS.
YOU WERE THE TARGET.

OUT WITH THE OLD, IN WITH THE NEW. THEY JUST DIDN'T FIGURE ON ME SMELLING A SETUP.
I BEEN IN WORSE CLUSTERFUCKS THAN THIS.

YOU GOT GOOD CHOPS, KID. YOU TOOK THE SHOT. I SAW YOU IN THE BUILDING, BUT DIDN'T MAKE YOU FOR A KILLER. WHERE'D YOU TRAIN?
MARINE CORPS. IRAQ FOR TWO TOURS. YOU?
THREE TOURS IN VIETNAM. SOMETIMES I WISH I'D STAYED IN. BUT I WAS SICK OF FIGHTING IN THE JUNGLE. TOO MANY BUGS.
I DIDN'T LIKE THE DESERT. TOO MUCH SAND.

IT WAS EITHER THIS--OR SPECIAL FORCES CROSSING INTO PAKISTAN. I'D RATHER BE HERE. SLATE'S HOME.
YEAH, I COULD HAVE GONE INTO CAMBODIA WITH RANGERS, OR COME BACK TO SLATE. I GREW UP HERE.

THE SMART THING FOR ME TO DO IS KILL YOU. BUT SOMETIMES IT'S NOT ENOUGH TO BE SMART.
YOU HAVE TO GO SPOOKY.

TELL MR. MACHINE YOU KILLED ME. I'LL DISAPPEAR, AND HE'LL HIRE YOU TO TAKE MY PLACE.
GOOD PLAN. SIMPLE AND EXPEDIENT.

JUST REMEMBER, KID. THEY'LL COME AFTER YOU ONE DAY. THEY'LL TRY TO FLUSH YOU OUT WITH A TRICK-- LIKE THEY TRIED WITH ME.
ALTER YOUR PATTERNS. DON'T KEEP YOUR MONEY IN ONE PLACE. GET A ROCK-HARD SET OF FALSE I.D.

ANY MORE LESSONS?
NO, KID, YOU'RE A NATURAL.

BLAM!

LESSON NUMBER ONE: FUCK YOU, DOG DICK.

LESSON TWO: NEVER UNDERESTIMATE THE ENEMY.

IT'S DONE.
NO. NO PROBLEMS AT ALL.
HE WAS JUST AN OLD MAN.
END

FRACTURE

ALEX DE CAMPI & HUGO PETRUS

NO.
NOT TODAY.

AXI
DING
HA
HA
HA
HA HA HA
HA
HA
HA

HAHAHAHA

HAHAHAHA

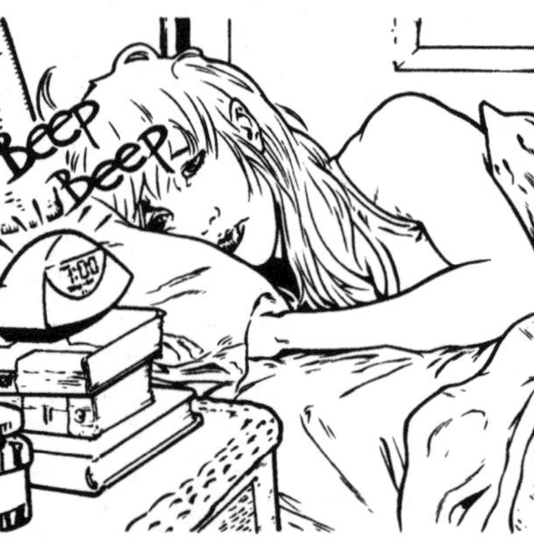
BEEP
BEEP

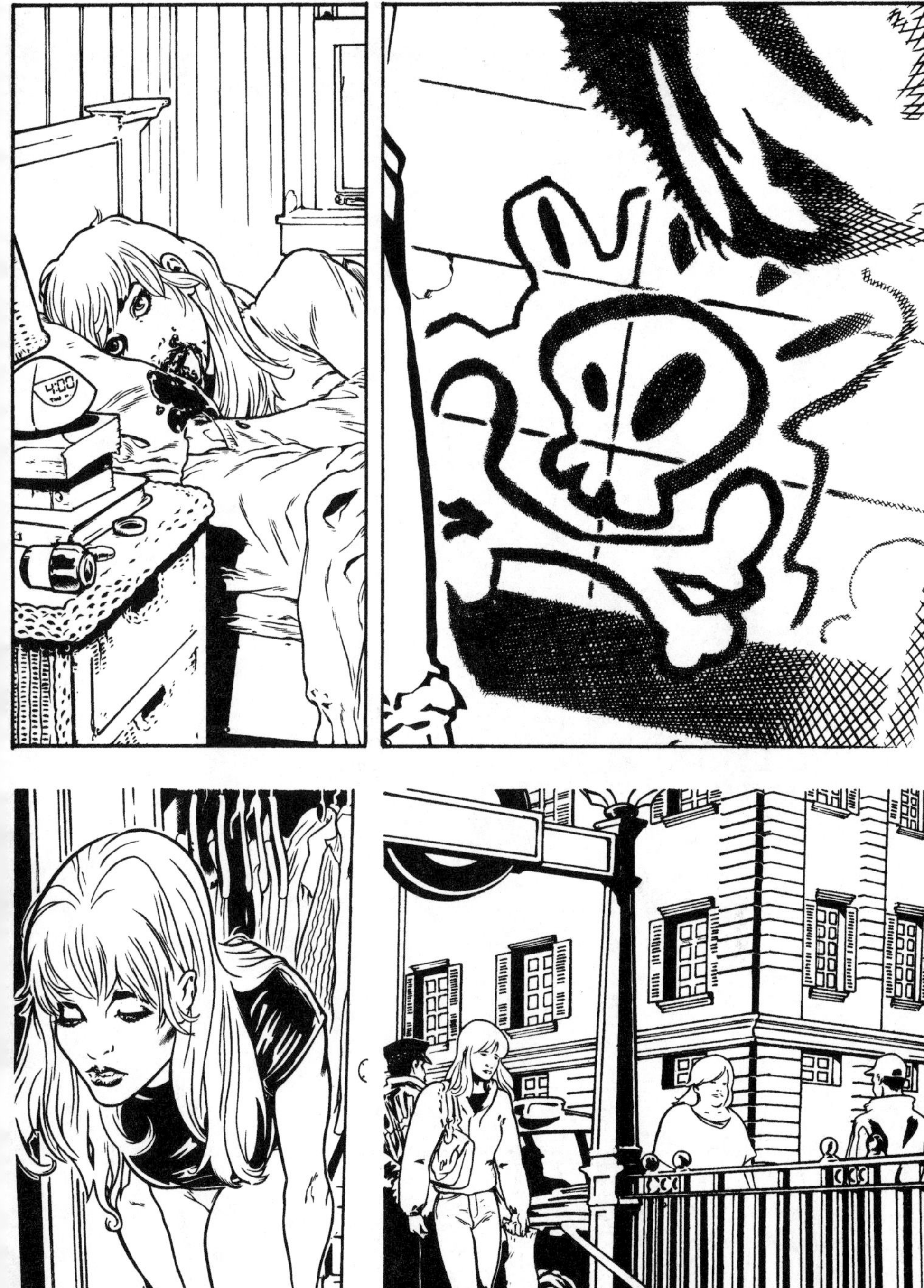
4:00

JES' A DOLLAH, GET ME SOMETHIN' TO EAT, C'MON, PRETTY, WASSAMATTAH, YOU DEAF?
DO YOU EVER THINK ABOUT IT? I THINK QUITE A LOT ABOUT IT.
IT WOULD BE SO EASY...
THE END

NO! COME ON, SHE ACTUALLY SAID THAT?

HOW MANY TIMES HAVE I TOLD YOU NOT TO WHISTLE ON MY SHIFT? YOU'VE GOT SIX MORE FLOORS, AND IT'S ALREADY 3:00 A.M., SO FINISH YOUR JOB IF YOU WANNA KEEP IT.

OH, JUST THE CLEANING GUY...HE DOESN'T SPEAK ENGLISH WELL. HE'S ALBANIAN... OR GREEK... DON'T KNOW.

The ALBANIAN

Written & Illustrated by

M. K. PERKER

HOLY MOSES!

HOLY SWEET MOSES!
IT SMELLS... BUT... BUT... NOT LIKE BLOOD.

IT SMELLS LIKE SHIT...

WHAT THE F--?!

OH! OH, NO! RUN...
I HAVE TO RUN NOW... REMEMBER WHAT COMMANDER AVNI USED TO SAY.

"IF YOU DON'T HEAR GUNSHOTS, BUT DO SEE PEOPLE WHO'VE BEEN SHOT--

"--RUN!" SHOULD I GRAB A CHAIR?

MAYBE I CAN USE IT AGAINST THE SHOOTER.
NO... THESE CHAIRS ALL HAVE WHEELS... HOW AM I GONNA USE THEM?

HEY! WHO'S THERE?
I CAN HEAR YOUR FOOTSTEPS, NIGHT-SHIFT GUY.
DON'T TRY TO RUN AWAY!
REMEMBER WHAT COMMANDER AVNI USED TO SAY...
"ALWAYS RUN IN THE DIRECTION YOU CAME FROM."
BUT WHAT IF SOMETHING HAPPENS IN THE ELEVATOR?
STAIRS... STAIRS ARE ALWAYS SAFER...

I KNEW IT WAS YOU. COME IN.

DON'T WORRY. WE'RE BOTH EXPATRIATES. WELL, NOT EXACTLY... MY GRANDMOTHER WAS SERBIAN.

AND SHE USED TO SPEAK SERBIAN TO US. HER ENGLISH WAS NO GOOD-- MY COUSINS AND I MADE FUN OF HER ALL THE TIME. OH... I'M SORRY. HOW RUDE OF ME...

OTHERWISE, HOW WOULD I RECOGNIZE YOU, RIGHT? BECAUSE I WORK IN THE OFFICE 'TIL MIDNIGHT MOST DAYS, AND I SEE YOU... WELL, MOSTLY I HEAR YOU.

YOU WHISTLE THAT SAME TUNE. IT'S PROBABLY SOME BALKAN FOLK SONG, I ASSUME.

I'M SORRY, SIR, WHAT? OH, IT'S IMPORTANT?

YES, SIR...HMM... I UNDERSTAND, SIR...YOU'RE ABSOLUTELY RIGHT.

WELL... BOSS SAYS WE HAVE TO FINISH THE JOB BEFORE MORNING. THERE'S ONE MORE FILE TO CLOSE.

I APOLOGIZE, BUT I HAVE TO GET BACK TO WORK.

WELL... NICE SEEING YOU... 'BYE NOW...

THIS GUY FROM ACCOUNTING GOES CRAZY, SHOOTS EVERYONE ON THE FLOOR, THEN SHOOTS HIMSELF IN THE HEAD. WE GOT THE CALL FROM THE NIGHT-SHIFT MANAGER. ONE OF HIS GUYS--ALBANIAN... OR TURKISH... I'M NOT SURE--FINDS THE BODIES AND INFORMS HIS BOSS. THEN THE MANAGER CALLS 9-1-1.

POOR GUY WAS STILL SHAKING WHEN WE GOT HERE. HIS ENGLISH IS PRETTY BAD.

TAKE HIM HOME NOW. HE'S HAD ENOUGH FOR TONIGHT. WE'VE ALREADY GOT HIS STATEMENT. LET'S GO OVER *IT* AND THE MANAGER'S.
THE GUY HAD A SILENCER. SO HE'D PROBABLY BEEN PLANNING THIS FOR A WHILE. GOING CRAZY IS A GRADUAL THING.

POLICE
THIS'S THE ADDRESS. PULL OVER, MIKE. ALL RIGHT, SIR. HAVE A GOOD NIGHT NOW.

211

<I TOLD YOU NOT TO WHISTLE WHEN YOU COME HOME. YOU'RE GONNA WAKE THE BOY UP!>
<HE'S SLEEPING. HEY, REMEMBER THE ACTION FIGURE HE WANTED FOR HIS BIRTHDAY THAT WE COULDN'T GET?>

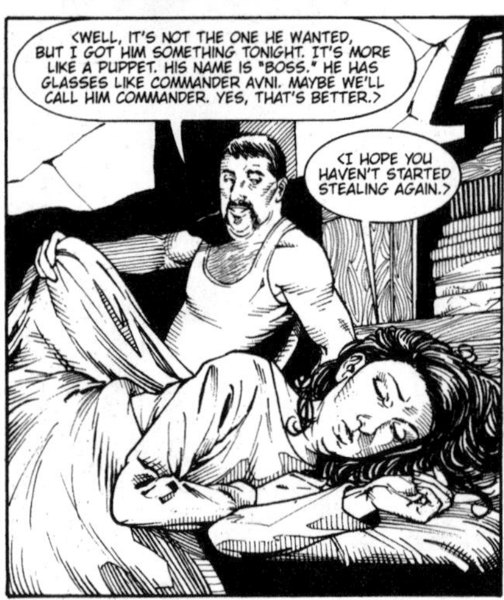
<WELL, IT'S NOT THE ONE HE WANTED, BUT I GOT HIM SOMETHING TONIGHT. IT'S MORE LIKE A PUPPET. HIS NAME IS "BOSS." HE HAS GLASSES LIKE COMMANDER AVNI. MAYBE WE'LL CALL HIM COMMANDER. YES, THAT'S BETTER.>
<I HOPE YOU HAVEN'T STARTED STEALING AGAIN.>

<WHO SAID ANYTHING ABOUT STEALING? YOU KNOW I'M DONE WITH THAT. WE CAME HERE TO HAVE A BETTER LIFE, AND I'M NOT GONNA RUIN IT. I LEFT ISTANBUL IN ISTANBUL.>
ZZZ...

fundit...
(The End)

WHEEOOP
THE OWNER ARRIVED BACK FROM AN OVERNIGHT TRIP TO FIND HIS APARTMENT BURGLED.
LIZ IS WITH HIM NOW, COMPILING A LIST OF STOLEN ITEMS.
AND YOU RECKON THIS IS OUR GUY, LUCY?
THE PLAYING-CARD BURGLAR?
POLICE
KANE
THE CARD PLAYER

oh YEAH. WE FOUND THE CARD.
WHY DO THEY ALL SEEM TO THINK THEY NEED A GIMMICK NOWADAYS?
EVERY-BODY WANTS TO THINK THEY'RE IN A FILM. ME? I'M ANGELINA JOLIE.
HE'S A BUSY GUY. THIS IS THE FIFTH JOB HE'S PULLED IN THE LAST WEEK.
SIXTH.
SO FAR WE'VE HAD FOUR REPORTED BURGLARIES IDENTIFIED WITH A PLAYING CARD.
ACE OF DIAMONDS, TWO, THREE, AND FOUR.
WHICH LEAVES US WITH THE QUESTION: WHAT HAPPENED TO NUMBER FIVE?

WELCOME TO EDGAR'S EMPORIUM... QUALITY GOODS AT BARGAIN PRICES!
ARE YOU LOOKING TO BUY OR SELL?
DETECTIVE KATE FELIX. NEW EDEN POLICE.
THIS IS MY COLLEAGUE DETECTIVE KANE.
YOU GAVE US A CALL, EDGAR ...
SAID YOU MIGHT HAVE COME ACROSS SOME STOLEN GOODS.
LOOK, DETECTIVES ...
I RUN AN HONEST SHOP HERE, BUT SOME-TIMES I THINK PEOPLE TAKE ADVANTAGE OF MY TRUSTING NATURE.
FOUR DAYS AGO, THIS KID, RON, HE COMES IN WITH THESE ANTIQUE VASES FROM HIS POOR DECEASED AUNT.
THE DAY BEFORE THAT IT WAS HIS GRANDMOTHER. POOR KID'S BEEN HAVING A BIT OF BAD LUCK WITH FAMILY MEMBERS OF LATE.
BUT I CAN'T HELP BUT THINK SOME-THING'S NOT RIGHT.
THEY CHECK OUT ON THE LIST OF ITEMS FROM THE SECOND BURGLARY.

AND YOU WAITED FOUR DAYS BEFORE CONTACTING THE POLICE ABOUT THIS?
WHAT CAN I SAY, DETECTIVE?
IT'S BEEN WEIGHING UPON MY CONSCIENCE.
DO YOU HAVE AN ADDRESS FOR RON? WE'D LIKE TO PASS ON OUR CONDOLENCES.
NO ...
BUT I GOT A PHONE NUMBER ...
THEY'RE GONE. YOU CAN COME OUT NOW.
I DON'T GET IT - I ALREADY GAVE YOU THE GUY'S DETAILS ...
WHY'D Y'NEED ME TO TELL THE COPS, TOO?
NEVER PLAY AN ACE WHEN A TWO WILL DO.

WHO'S THERE?

POLICE!

DONAHUE- HE'S HEADING WEST DOWN THE ALLEY. GREEN CHECK SHIRT, BLUE JEANS.

I SAW HIM DUCK IN HERE. WE'VE GOT UNITS COVERING EVERY EXIT.
THIS PLACE IS A WARREN. HE COULD BE ANY-WHERE.
FAN OUT. BE THOROUGH.

mmmf
SHHH!
uh
I'M SORRY, GUY.
NOTHING OVER HERE.

LOOKS LIKE WE LOST HIM ...
THAT COP—HE JUST LET ME GO!
HE EVEN APOLOGIZED ...
WAIT... I KNOW YOU...I'VE SEEN YOU IN THE PAPER.
YOU'RE OSCAR DARKE ...
THEY SAY YOU'RE THE CRIME BOSS OF NEW EDEN...
MISTER DARKE WANTS A WORD WITH YOU...
ME? WHY? WHAT'VE I DONE?

THIS YOUR GUY?
YEAH. SINGLE GUNSHOT WOUND TO THE HEAD.
LOOKS LIKE THEY GAVE HIM A GOOD GOING-OVER FIRST.
FOUND THIS NEXT TO THE BODY.
POLICE
WELL, I GUESS THAT'S "CASE CLOSED" FOR THE CARD BURGLAR.
AND WE NEVER FOUND THE FIFTH VICTIM.
NO.
BUT IT SEEMS OUR BURGLAR DID.
5
5
END

BLOOD ON MY HANDS

RICK GEARY
©07

I'VE BEEN ITCHING TO TELL THIS STORY FOR QUITE SOME TIME, ALTHOUGH IT REFLECTS UPON ME POORLY.

I HAD BEEN MARRIED FOR ABOUT FIVE YEARS TO CARLA — A WOMAN OF RARE AND INCANDESCENT SPIRIT.

TO OTHERS, SHE MIGHT NOT HAVE SEEMED MUCH OF A "CATCH," BUT I MADE OF HER THE REPOSITORY OF MY PASSION.

TO THIS SHE WAS AGREEABLE ENOUGH.

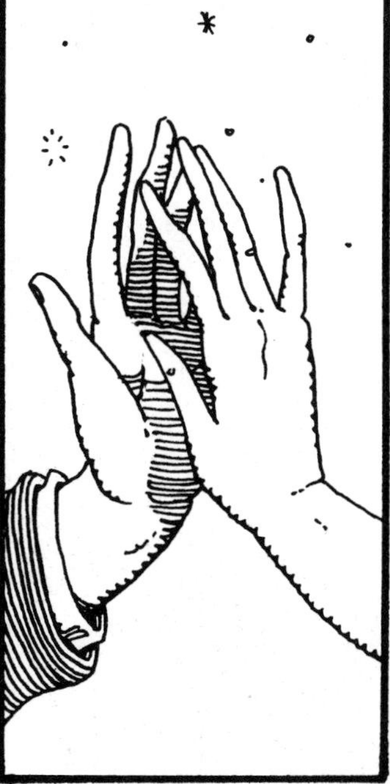

WE WERE CONTENT TO JUST SIT HOME OF AN EVENING AND WATCH TELEVISION.

EVERYTHING CHANGED WHEN I LOST MY JOB AT THE DEALERSHIP.

AT THAT TIME, THE ENTIRE LOCAL ECONOMY WAS TAKING A PLUNGE.

I TRIED IN EVERY WAY I COULD TO FIND EMPLOYMENT.
JOBS
JOBS
JOBS
I GOT MINE!
JOBS
JOBS
JOBS

AT LAST I FELT TOO HUMILIATED TO LEAVE THE HOUSE.

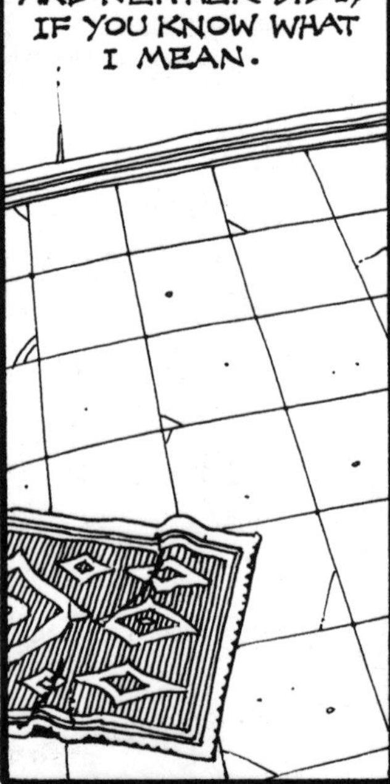
I STARED AT THE FLOORS AND THE WALLS. LIFE HELD NO JUICE, AND NEITHER DID I, IF YOU KNOW WHAT I MEAN.

CARLA INSISTED I SEE A DOCTOR—ONE WHO SPECIALIZED IN JUST SUCH A CONDITION AS MINE.

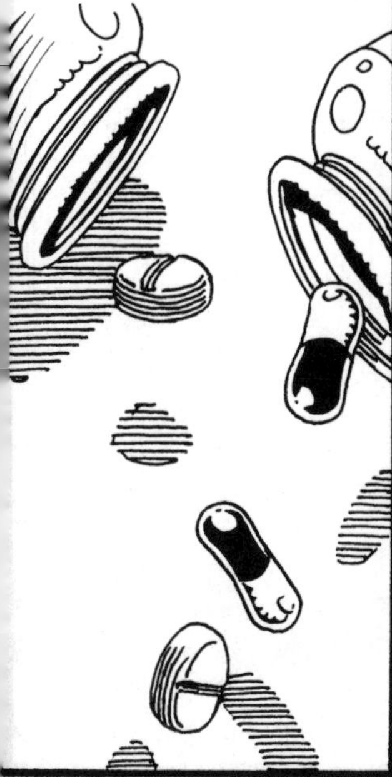
HE PRESCRIBED TWO KINDS OF PILLS — ONE RED AND ONE A BRIGHT AQUAMARINE.

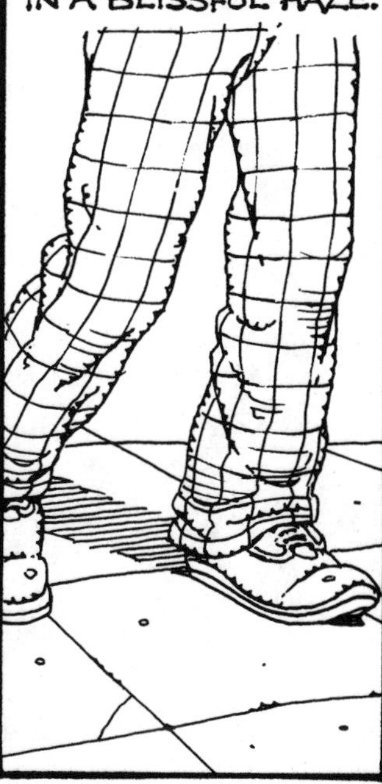
I TOOK EACH ONE TWICE A DAY. FOR A WHILE, I WENT ABOUT IN A BLISSFUL HAZE.

IN THE MEANTIME, CARLA FOUND OFFICE WORK WITH AN INSURANCE COMPANY DOWNTOWN.

HER WORK KEPT HER LATE ON MANY NIGHTS, BUT THAT DIDN'T BOTHER ME.

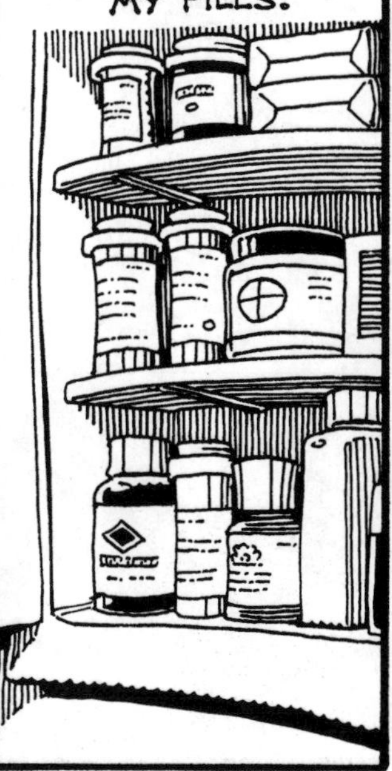
I FELT SO FINE, IN FACT, THAT I THOUGHT I MAY AS WELL STOP TAKING MY PILLS.

AND IT WASN'T LONG BEFORE THE HAZE GAVE WAY TO A PRICKLY, JINGLY, HEEDLESS SENSATION.

I COULD FEEL CARLA DETACHING HERSELF. ONE NIGHT SHE MISSED DINNER ALTOGETHER.

AND WHEN SHE APPEARED, SHE WAS ALL SMILES AND APOLOGIES.

DID SHE EVER LOVE ME AT ALL? THE SHAME WAS GREATER THAN I COULD BEAR.

SO I CONSULTED A PRIVATE INVESTIGATOR. WE MET AT A NEARBY COFFEE SHOP.
Chicken Fried Steak
* $7.00

HE ASKED ME IF I WAS PREPARED TO KNOW THE TRUTH, BECAUSE IT MIGHT NOT BE PRETTY.

I PAID HIM IN ADVANCE FOR TWO WEEKS' INVESTIGATION.
DOLLARS

AT THE END OF THAT TIME, HE PRESENTED ME WITH A DETAILED REPORT.

ON CERTAIN DAYS, ACCORDING TO THE REPORT, MY WIFE WOULD LEAVE THE INSURANCE OFFICE IN THE COMPANY OF A MAN.

701

THEY WOULD DRIVE OFF IN HIS LATE-MODEL CAR.

THE INVESTIGATOR WOULD THEN FOLLOW THEM TO A MOTEL.
Shamrock
MOTEL

THEY ALTERNATED AMONG SEVERAL LOCAL ESTABLISHMENTS.
CITY CENTER
LODGE

WHO WAS THE MAN? THAT HARDLY MATTERS. HE WOULD REGISTER UNDER A FALSE NAME.

WHEN I ASKED THE INVESTIGATOR TO PHONE ME THE NEXT TIME THEY CHECKED IN, HE QUESTIONED MY INTENTIONS.

I TOLD HIM THAT I WANTED TO SEE THE LOOK ON HER FACE WHEN SHE EMERGED FROM THE ROOM AND FOUND ME JUST STANDING THERE.

IN REALITY, THOUGH, I HAD BY THAT TIME SPOKEN WITH A PROFESSIONAL ASSASSIN.

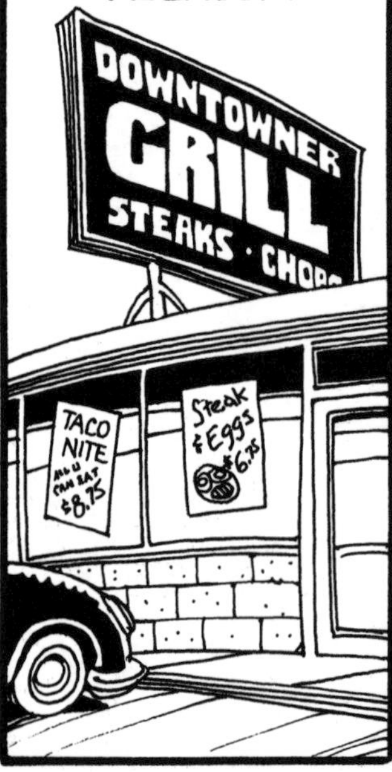

BELIEVE ME, ONE HAS TO JUMP THROUGH HOOPS THESE DAYS JUST TO SECURE A MEETING. HE SEEMED A NICE ENOUGH GUY, THOUGH.

HE SUGGESTED A SHOTGUN, SINCE THERE WOULD BE NO BULLET TO TRACE.

HOW COULD I HAVE INITIATED SUCH A CHAIN OF EVENTS? NO DOUBT I WAS OFF MY MEDS IN A BIG WAY.

ONE DAY, THE INVESTIGATOR CALLED TO LET ME KNOW MY WIFE'S LOCATION.

AT ONCE, I SIGNALED THE ASSASSIN.

I THEN SPENT THE DAY IN INNOCENT PURSUITS. I MOWED THE LAWN.

I EXCHANGED PLEASANTRIES WITH THE NEIGHBOR LADY.

NEVER BEFORE HAD I BEEN SUCH A FRIENDLY, TALKATIVE FELLOW.

THAT NIGHT ON THE NEWS, THERE WAS A REPORT ABOUT A COUPLE MURDERED IN A MOST GHASTLY MANNER AT A LOCAL MOTEL.

WAIT A MINUTE! WAS THAT THE RIGHT PLACE?
TROPICANA
INN
REST
BEST WESTERN

AT THAT MOMENT, SHE WALKED IN THE DOOR.

DON'T ASK ME HOW IT HAPPENED. OBVIOUSLY A MAJOR MISCOMMUNICATION.

SINCE THEN, CARLA AND I ARE INTIMATE AS NEVER BEFORE. I'M BACK AT THE DEALERSHIP.

THANKS FOR LISTENING. I FEEL MUCH BETTER.

TRU$TWORTHY

***written by* KEN LIZZI*, illustrated by* JOËLLE JONES**

It didn't get deadly until near the end. The scene played out in a dark, smoky, rock-and-roll club—Downrange—lively, with an undercurrent of danger. The joint drew an eclectic clientele: a mélange of hipsters, young professionals, and young professional criminals. A three-piece combo wailed a driving blues jam.

But that comes later. First, some introductions.

Cleveland—black on black: a dark-skinned man in black slacks and dress shirt topped by a black leather jacket. Palpably menacing; savagery lurking beneath a smooth veneer of urbanity. Law and convention no restraint. A patron of Downrange.

Sonja—sleek, a Mediterranean beauty. She moves like a satiated hunting cat, graceful and unconcerned, and just as amoral. She had good reason to steer clear of Downrange the night it went down.

And then there's Ray, the hero of the piece. Thirty or thereabouts (it's not important), a nine-to-fiver, stable, until recently as happy as anyone.

That runs down the main players. Extras will go unnamed. Now, to back up a bit, start this thing properly.

Work, hit the gym, shower. It was a Friday night, which meant a little R&R. Ray needed to leave work at the office where it belonged. Leave behind talk of broken promises and "limiting options to upper management only." He hit a pub for a burger and a beer, maybe four. A band was setting up its equipment against the back wall. Friday night traffic began trickling in.

Ray didn't notice her enter. He hailed the bartender, calling for his third frosty pill. Sensing a presence approach, he turned to see this exotic creature mount the bar stool to his right. With long, elegant fingers she drew a cigarette from the pack. Ray nabbed a pack of matches from the bar and sparked the coffin nail as she placed it between full, darkly red lips.

"My hero," she said, exhaling a stream of smoke. "You know, I only smoke when I drink?" It came out a question.

He took the hint. "What'll you have?" he asked. Then, dropping a couple more bills onto the stained, hardwood surface of the bar, relayed her preference to the bartender.

"Ray," he offered, extending a hand.

"Sonja," she replied, giving him her fingers for a brief clasp. "So, Ray, will you tell me all about being Ray?" She leaned near, her gaze fixed and intense. If he'd had a prescient bone in his body, he'd have noticed an air of desperation as well. Hindsight—it's like owning prime real estate on the moon, an essentially useless possession.

Later, Ray could recall little of the band that played that night, nor much of the conversation. He tried to dress up the drudgery of administrative work at the lab, hint at hush-hush work on the holography project as if he actually had a hand in. Now was not the time to dwell on reality—middle-management hell and last-minute backstabbing. She was not forthcoming about herself. He didn't push. Gift horse and all that. There were drinks, a slow dance, cash replaced by plastic, then more drinks. When they reached Ray's condo (located just within the city limits, not quite in the 'burbs), they'd played out of conversation. In bed she clutched at him, arms wrapped around his back as if it were an airline seat cushion and sex the event of a water landing. Afterwards she continued to clasp him to her, like a last straw.

She was still there in the morning. He didn't mind. The rapid seduction and the concomitant rapid departure of the one-night stand, which he'd thought she'd intended, no longer held great allure. He was not opposed to a one-nighter, and he certainly would not turn it down, but he no longer lettered in that sport.

So he was pleased to see her lying next to him. The pleasure, unfortunately, was short-lived.

He rose to cook breakfast, ignoring the symptoms of a mild hangover. Coffee had begun to percolate when the front door reverberated from the repeated poundings of a fist. It was not a polite knock. He made a brief detour to the bedroom, snagging the Beretta 9mm from the nightstand before assaying the situation at the front door.

A peep through the peephole revealed a fish-eye view of a sharply dressed black man. Snug dark sport coat, tan on tan shirt-and-tie combo. At this time on a Saturday morning?

"What do you want?" Ray called, loudly enough to be heard through the solid core door.

Apparently he wanted to know if anyone was home. A low-topped boot drew back, then the heel slammed against the door, just below the handle. The dead bolt held. The heel drew back again. Ray turned the dead bolt, jerked open the door and thrust the pistol within inches of the man's face. The heel stopped.

"Now, you tell me who you are and why you're scuffing up the paint on my front door." Ray doubted that he sounded as calm as he'd hoped.

He envied how quickly the unexpected visitor collected himself. He drew his gaze away from the muzzle of the automatic and focused on Ray's face. He took a short breath and rolled his neck like a fighter before a bout. A good bet that he'd had a gun pointed at him before. Ray'd had grouchy R&D techs point angry fingers at him, but that's about as far as his familiarity with aggro extended.

"I know Sonja is inside," the man began quietly. "Now I'm gonna give you a break. You got picked up for a place to stay. You don't know nothing. So I'm not gonna take this personal. You just tell that bitch I want my money. No more games, no more chasing her ass around. She don't need to come out right now. You can play hero for a while longer. But I want it tonight. At the club."

He raised his voice, no longer speaking quietly. "You hear that, Sonja? You bring the money to the club tonight! All of it! Not a hunner'-ninety-eight Gs, not a hunner'-ninety-nine Gs. All two hundred motherfuckin' thousand dollars!"

He refocused on Ray. "And you. If she don't show tonight, boy, your hall pass is expired."

He turned and strode off. Ray's rejoinder of "Have a nice day" fell flat.

So much for the pleasant morning. Death threats and vast amounts of ill-gotten cash did not form a part of Ray's life. Excitement in his life consisted of being on the administrative periphery of the scientific cutting edge, and, more meaningful to Ray, talk of IPOs and employee stock options—talk which had recently turned bitter in his mouth.

The impact of the encounter at his front door hit home. He began to feel a bit queasy, and doubted it was the hangover. Another bit of unpleasantness was now inevitable.

"You hear all of that?" he asked, closing the front door.

Sonja emerged from the bedroom, hair tousled, clad in one of Ray's dress shirts. She nodded. "I heard. You're not too mad, are you? I needed a place to hide for the night, right? But I wouldn't have come home with you if I didn't like you. You know that, don't you? I would have . . ." She stalled.

Ray finished for her. "Would have found another lonely sucker."

"That's not fair! You think I used you? Maybe a little," she admitted. "But how can you attack me like this when you don't know what's going on? You don't know why. And it's not like you didn't get anything out of it. Didn't you have a good time last night?"

"Maybe I'll remember after I get over having my life threatened by a big, angry pimp."

"His name's Cleveland. What makes you think he's a pimp? He's a drug dealer."

"Oh. My bad. Sorry to impugn his character."

"You think I'm a prostitute?" Her indignation sounded forced. "I told you I wouldn't have come home with you if I didn't like you. Sure I was desperate, but I could have found a hotel, or the bus station, or something, right?"

He had to relent a bit. He was unwilling to believe she'd just happened to fall for him, Mr. Right, in the course of her flight from the badass Cleveland. But in fairness, he had yet to hear her out.

"Look, you go take a shower. I'll finish cooking breakfast. Then you can tell me your story."

She was halfway through her plate of scrambled eggs when she began. "I'm a courier. Not exactly legit though, know what I mean? I carry money, that's all I do. That's not so bad, is it? Cleveland sets up these deals. He tells me where to go, who to meet. Someone hands over money. When I get the money, I make a phone call to Cleveland's pager. He completes the deal, hands over the stuff, whatever it happens to be. Why would I want to know? Better off not knowing. Then I bring him the cash.

"Two nights ago I didn't make the call. I pretended to—you know, just punched my home digits, right? It was easy. I walked away with the money, stopped in a public restroom, and transferred the money to my purse, that oversize shoulder bag I carry, see? You know how compact a hundred bundles of twenty one-hundred-dollar bills really is? Fit right, snug, like the purse was made just for that purpose. I think that's why I did it. I hadn't planned on keeping the money. You believe me, right? It was always at the back of my mind, but how could I make it practical? Usually payment is in, what, twenties and tens? Bulky. I'd have to plan and prepare in advance. I never was serious enough to do it—too afraid of Cleveland. But this time, this time it looked so easy. I looked down at all that money, and I just couldn't stop myself. I figured I could just walk away, get out of town. Maybe start a new life?"

She paused, listlessly stirring the eggs on her plate. "I suppose I should have known better. Cleveland never would have trusted me with the money if he hadn't been sure he could track me down. Maybe I assumed he was in love with me—a big, dopey, dangerous dog who trusted me and who I could take advantage of."

"Why would you think he was in love with you?" Ray asked, keeping his eyes on his plate.

"You mean, was I sleeping with him? Yes, of course. Me and half of the female population of the metro area. Why I thought I was special I can't say now. But despite all the other women, I guess we both felt that sex sealed a bond of trust—to a point. Using each other to our mutual advantage is probably a better description of the relationship. I never loved him, and like I said, he apparently never loved me."

Looking at Sonja, Ray felt chilled. There sat Amorality, eating eggs at his kitchen table.

"What do you propose to do now?" he asked.

She looked up at him, eyes wide, kittenish, frightened. "I was hoping you would ask, 'What do you propose *we* do now?'"

Amazing. So mutable. No segue from cold manipulator to—well, to warm, vulnerable manipulator.

He rose, poured himself another cup of mud, and sat back down. "Would you, by any chance, have a suggestion?" He delivered the line as evenly, as neutrally as he could.

Pushing aside her plate, she leaned across the table. "You're not a player, right? Your hands aren't dirty. You have a good face. When I first sat down next to you, I could tell you were honest, trustworthy. Cleveland can read that just as well as I could. He'd never believe you could be anything but a straight shooter."

He waited. He had some inkling where she was going with this whitewash.

"Say you bring Cleveland the money," she continued, "just not all of it. Have you been to Downrange? The club? It's not well lit. In the dark a bundle of cut paper looks just like a bundle of cash if there's a real bill on top. Cleveland would never suspect, not immediately. You'd have time to get out of there. *We'd* have time to get out of town. Two people can go a long way on nearly two hundred Gs." She ran her hand gently along the side of Ray's face as she spoke these last words, gazing directly into his eyes.

"He said he wanted *you*," he temporized.

"What he wants is the money, right? If he thinks he has that, he won't care if I don't show. Please, baby, we can be together. Think about it." She pulled Ray's face down to hers, and ceased attempting to persuade him with words.

That afternoon Ray sat snipping at paper, producing regular, rectangular piles. He sent Sonja out to buy a new purse, saying his performance would be more convincing if he delivered the phony package in her purse. He made a brief trip while she was out. It was early evening by the time she returned.

He showed her his handiwork: her purse packed with what appeared to be stacks of cash.

"And the rest?" she asked.

He parted the top folds of a towel-wrapped bundle resting on top of the kitchen table, revealing more rubber-banded stacks.

"Let me have your new purse," he demanded.

She handed over a large shoulder bag. He lowered the bundle in. "Good fit. Now, I recommend we get some rest. We'll be on the move all night once I pull this off—if I pull this off."

She grabbed his hand. "Don't doubt yourself. You can't fail."

They lay in the semi-darkness of the bedroom, Sonja once more running through her plan, describing the layout of the club and the location of Cleveland's reserved table. Ray tried to minimize his visualization of the night's possible events and outcome. Every instinct, all reason dictated that he call the police and bolt the door. But each time he felt his nerves reach the breaking point, he conjured up images of his motivation, and squeezed Sonja's hand reassuringly.

At roughly midnight he stood ready to leave the condo. A long overcoat concealed Sonja's purse. Underneath the overcoat a sport coat concealed his nine-millimeter pistol. He performed a tolerable job of not shaking.

By the front door sat Sonja's new purse, next to a duffle bag he'd packed.

Sonja kissed him deeply. "You know I'll be waiting, right? I trust you."

"I trust you. Turn the deadbolt. Don't open the door for anyone but me."

So, there he stood in the doorway of Downrange—a dark, smoky, rock-and-roll club, with an eclectic clientele: a mélange of hipsters, young professionals, and young professional criminals. Anyway, Ray was a young professional, Cleveland was a criminal, and hipsters danced to a three-piece combo wailing a driving blues jam.

Cleveland sat where Sonja said he'd be, in a secluded booth near the rear exit.

"Where the fuck's Sonja?" he greeted Ray, loud enough to be heard over the music.

Ray opened up his overcoat to reveal the purse. He sat down at the booth across from Cleveland and set the purse on the table between them, then dropped his hands to his lap. "She couldn't make it. Headache, I think."

"Don't fuck with me, hero. This isn't a game."

"Fine. Do you want the money? It's here. Sonja's not."

"Yeah. I want the money." He poked the barrel of a pistol over the tabletop. "How do you like that? A little payback for this morning. Now, you sit still while I do some counting."

Cleveland pulled the purse toward him. Ray pulled the trigger of the pistol he'd had trained on Cleveland. The muzzle flash beneath the table splashed brief shadows through the rear of the club. Cleveland jerked back against his chair without a sound, the arm tugging the purse flung wide. The shot broke the relentless drive of the music, which faltered, relented. Ray ran out through the back door amidst a fluttering shower of paper.

Ray reflected as he drove home, mildly surprised that he felt so little after killing a man. He'd supposed he would experience remorse, crippling guilt, or perhaps even elation. He felt nothing. He'd squashed spiders that had elicited greater regret. Ray wondered what this said about him.

He slowed the car as he crossed the river. Lowering the passenger window, he tossed the pistol out, over the bridge railing into the darkness below.

The door to his condominium was unlocked. Sonja's new purse was gone. So was his duffle bag. Ray supposed she'd needed a few things for the road.

He went into the bedroom, knelt down, and pulled a suitcase from beneath the bed. Opening the suitcase, he lifted aside some clothing and a few other things for the road. Neatly stacked piles of $100 bills nestled where he'd placed them that afternoon.

Sure, he'd trusted Sonja. Trusted her to use *him* just as she'd used Cleveland. Trusted her to misjudge him as badly as she'd misjudged Cleveland. Cleveland hadn't believed Ray was honest and trustworthy. But Sonja had.

The compact holographic projector he'd placed in Sonja's new purse was a marketing sample, not a prototype, so it wasn't worth its weight in money, though it did conveniently weigh roughly the same as the "money" in the purse he'd passed to Cleveland. The company had long passed the prototype phase. The sample would be missed, but its loss wasn't fatal to the company, not that Ray cared any longer. Figured it was payback for the way he'd been treated.

The holographic projection of bundled stacks of cash was much more convincing than cut strips of newspaper topped with a single bill. At least it would be until Sonja tried to reach for a stack and found her hand passing through thin air. Sonja was a resourceful girl, and given time to think about it might consider this a fair trade—a sample of a technology that had yet to hit the market could have significant value to the right parties. But he'd rigged the projector with a patent protection device, i.e., a self-destruct, so Sonja wouldn't be selling the soon-to-be-fused mass of plastic, circuits, and glass to a competitor. True, Ray could have gone the espionage route himself, given enough lead time to plan. But considering the abruptness of the whole mess, he'd just as soon take the cash. So why the self-destruct, why leave Sonja holding the short straw? Residual company loyalty? Laziness? Maybe he was second-guessing his own motivations, but he reckoned it was pure spite. The reason was no longer important.

Screw this crashing dot-com economy, Ray thought. I'm strictly cash-and-carry now. He picked up the suitcase. Time to hit the road.

THE NEW ME
by Phillips/Barreto
"THERE HE IS, ALL SINEW AND ENCOURAGEMENT, WHISTLING WHILE HE WORKS THE BODIES. HELPING THE SOCCER MOMS AND CAREER GALS FEEL THE BURN.
"AND FOR CERTAIN CLIENTS, RUMOR HAS IT, HE OFFERS VERY PERSONAL OFF-HOURS ATTENTION...
"...TO HELP THE LADIES STAY IN SHAPE.
"SUCH A BUSY MAN, SO MANY WOMEN TO TRAIN, SO LITTLE TIME TO SHOWER IN BETWEEN.
"I WONDER: DOES HE NEED A BOOST FROM VIAGRA? CIALIS? OR IS IT JUST SHEER WILLPOWER THAT GETS THE JOB DONE?
"THOUGH IT'S NOT LIKE I'M HERE TO FIND THAT OUT..."

HI, I'M CHAD REYNOLDS, THE LEAD TRAINER HERE. I UNDERSTAND YOU WANT TO GET IN SHAPE, AND I WANT TO HELP YOU MAKE THAT HAPPEN.
SUSAN, ISN'T IT?
YES--SUSAN MACY. GOOD TO MEET YOU, MR. REYNOLDS.
CALL ME CHAD, SUSAN. WE CERTAINLY AREN'T SLAVES TO FORMALITY AT THIS FACILITY. BESIDES, WE'LL BE WORKING CLOSELY TOGETHER TO HELP YOU ACHIEVE OPTIMUM RESULTS.
I'D JUST LIKE TO, YOU KNOW, GET TONED UP.
TONED UP IS JUST THE FIRST PHASE OF WHAT I'M GOING TO DO FOR YOU. SPIN CLASS, WEIGHT REGIME, NUTRITION, SOME SWIMMING-- WE'RE TALKING A NEW YOU.
UM... OKAY... SURE.
THAT'S THE SPIRIT! NOW COME ON, LET'S DO SOME STRETCHES TO GET YOU WARMED UP. PREPARATION IS EVERYTHING.

A FEW DAYS LATER.
THAT'S IT, SUSAN--MOVE TO THE GROOVE! KEEP THOSE KNEES PUMPING. WE'RE WORKING THE LEGS AND THE HEART, AND YOUR STOMACH WILL THANK YOU FOR IT.
OOOF! OOOF! GREAT.
THAT'S IT, NINE, TEN... COME ON, GIVE ME FIVE MORE.
OH, CHADDY, COULD YOU HELP ME WITH MY SQUATS?
UH, SUZE, KEEP GOING, OKAY? I'LL BE RIGHT BACK.
"SURE, HIS ATTENTION WAS ALWAYS DIVIDED WHEN IT CAME TIME FOR MY WORKOUTS. BUT IT DID *MATTER* THAT HE GAVE ME POINTERS AND SHOWED ME THE CORRECT WAY TO USE THE MACHINES."
KEEP STROKING, SUSAN, KEEP STROKING.
I'VE GOT A STROKE FOR YOU, CHAD. HEH.
"AFTER A WHILE, I GOT USED TO OUR SESSIONS. HE'D GIVE ME HIS CANNED PEP TALK, THEN I'D TUNE OUT WHATEVER GYM-RAT BIMBO HE WAS HITTING ON, AND CONCENTRATE ON MY WORKOUT.
"AND I DID START TO SEE *RESULTS.*"

FIVE WEEKS LATER.
HUH.
WHAT IS IT, BABY?
I THOUGHT I SAW SOME-BODY I KNOW. ONE OF MY CLIENTS.
YEAH, WELL, I'M YOUR CLIENT RIGHT NOW. AND YOU'D BETTER BE SERVICING ME BEFORE MY HUSBAND GETS HOME.
YES, MA'AM!
UMMMM, THAT'S BETTER!
DIDN'T I SEE YOU THE OTHER DAY WITH AN OLD GUY IN A WHEELCHAIR? THAT YOUR DAD OR SOMETHING?
OR SOMETHING. SEE YOU NEXT TUESDAY.

NEXT TUESDAY.
YOU KNOW, SUSAN, YOU'RE REALLY PROGRESSING WELL. I'M QUITE PLEASED WITH THE RESULTS.
I'M PLEASED, TOO. YOU'VE BEEN THERE FOR ME WHEN IT COUNTED.
I'D LIKE TO DO MORE, SUSAN. RELEASE MORE OF YOUR POTENTIAL.
REALLY?
I MEAN, YOU KNOW, YOU MUST BE, WELL...
FRUSTRATED? YOU CHECKED UP ON ME, RIGHT? YOU FOUND OUT THAT THE MAN IN THE WHEEL-CHAIR IS MY HUSBAND.
HEARD HE WAS SOME KIND OF PROF OVER AT THE UNIVERSITY. HE WAS ON HIS WAY UP UNTIL HE GOT SICK.
I WON'T PRETEND IT HASN'T BEEN HARD.
AND WHAT DROVE YOU TO THE GYM WAS SEEING WHAT HAPPENED TO HIM. YOU KNEW YOU HAD TO TAKE CARE OF YOURSELF.
DON'T YOU SEE, SUSAN? YOU CAN'T LET TIME SLIP PAST YOU WITHOUT TAKING FULL ADVANTAGE OF LIFE! WHO KNOWS WHAT'S IN STORE FOR ANY OF US?

THAT A VARIATION ON THE LINE YOU GIVE THE WOMEN AROUND HERE, CHAD?
IT ISN'T LIKE THAT, SUSAN. YOU AND ME--AND EVERY-ONE ELSE HERE--KNOW WHAT'S WHAT. I'M NOT PRETENDING TO BE SOMETHING I'M NOT. NO PROMISES, OTHER THAN MAKING US BOTH FEEL GOOD.
ALL ABOUT THE PHYSICAL?
I'M NOT THAT SHALLOW. BUT THERE'S NO DENYING THAT YOU TURN ME ON.
NOW THAT I'M NOT A DOG, YOU MEAN.
SUSAN...
SEE YOU THURSDAY, CHAD.

THREE MORE WEEKS GO BY.
I WON'T BE TOO LONG, DEAR.
WHAUUGHH.
SUSAN...
RELAX, BABY. I'M GOING TO GIVE YOU SOMETHING YOU'LL NEVER FORGET.
UGHHH.

DAMN, BITCH, YOU GOT SOME SHARP TEETH. WATCH THAT BITING, WOULD YOU?!
WHA...?
UH. MUST HAVE BEEN OUT. WHAT DID THAT FREAK DO TO ME? GOTTA GET UP, BUT WHY CAN'T I MOVE? DID SHE TIE ME UP?
YOU SEE, I NEEDED UPPER BODY STRENGTH TO MOVE YOU ONCE I'D KNOCKED YOU OUT. I ALREADY HAD A CAR PARKED AT THE MOTEL WE JUST "HAPPENED" TO WALK BY.
I GOT YOU BACK HERE TO OUR BASEMENT LAB. AND THANKS TO YOUR TRAINING, I WAS ABLE TO LIFT STEVE'S POOR BODY ONTO THE TABLE.
HUH?
SUSAN WAS MY ASSISTANT YEARS AGO, WHEN WE FELL IN LOVE. I'D BEEN WORKING ON THIS TRANSFERENCE METHOD, AND SHE CONTINUED MY WORK AFTER I HAD THE STROKE.
SORRY IT HAD TO COME TO THIS, CHAD. BUT I AM A LOYAL WIFE, AND WE DO HAVE A CRUISE SHIP TO CATCH.
THOSE WOMEN AT THE GYM WILL MISS YOU, BUT NO DOUBT THE NEXT TRAINER CAN HELP THEM GET OVER THAT.
THERE'S A RAMP LEADING TO THE OUTSIDE, DEAR. IT SHOULD ONLY TAKE YOU AN HOUR OR SO TO CRAWL INTO THE WHEELCHAIR.
WILL WHISTLE FOR FOOD
EDUARDO BARRETO
THE END

LADY'S CHOICE

BY THE FILLBÄCH BROTHERS

SHE WAS GETTING BORED AGAIN.

BORED WITH THIS CITY.

BORED WITH THIS LIFE.

FRANZ HELMUT. HE WAS OKAY... AT FIRST.

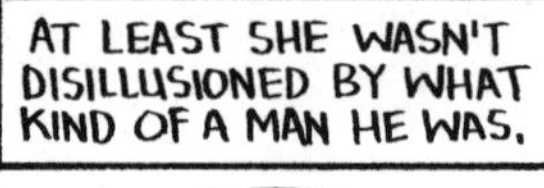
AT LEAST SHE WASN'T DISILLUSIONED BY WHAT KIND OF A MAN HE WAS.

SELF-CENTERED. OFTEN CRUEL. A MAN WHO TOOK WHAT HE WANTED.

A MAN OF QUESTIONABLE BUSINESS ETHICS. THE LESS SHE KNEW ABOUT HIS WORK, THE BETTER, SHE THOUGHT.

THINGS WERE FUN FOR A WHILE.

THE MONEY.

THE CLUBS.

BUT THE BOREDOM SET IN AGAIN, AND SHE WAS WAITING FOR SOMETHING NEW.

SHE WAITED FOR SOMEONE NEW...

SHE SAW HIM THE MOMENT HE WALKED THROUGH THE DOOR.

IF ANYONE SHOULD LOOK OUT OF PLACE HERE, IT WAS HIM, BUT...

...THEN AGAIN, HE DIDN'T SEEM OUT OF PLACE.
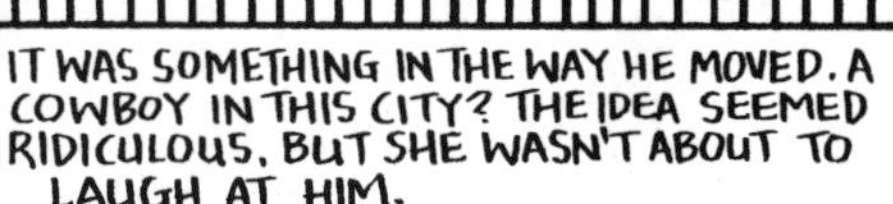
IT WAS SOMETHING IN THE WAY HE MOVED. A COWBOY IN THIS CITY? THE IDEA SEEMED RIDICULOUS, BUT SHE WASN'T ABOUT TO LAUGH AT HIM.

HE WALKED RIGHT UP, LOOKED HER IN THE EYES...
... AND SPOKE.

HER PULSE QUICKENED.

BUT IT WASN'T **HER** HE SPOKE TO.

FRANZ, I'VE COME FOR THE MONEY. GIVE IT TO ME, AND I'LL BE ON MY WAY.

HE WAS AN AMERICAN.

AN AMERICAN COWBOY.

SHE COULDN'T HELP BUT SMILE.

THE WAY HE SPOKE TO FRANZ.

TREATING HIM LIKE A CHILD.

TALKING DOWN TO HIM.

SHE LIKED THE WAY HE SPOKE.

HIS EYES ON HER, YET TALKING TO FRANZ.

COWBOY, YOU COME TO MY CLUB AND INSULT ME? I COULD HAVE YOU KILLED AND YOUR BODY NEVER FOUND.

THE MONEY.

FRANZ WAS NERVOUS. SHE COULD TELL. PUTTING ON HIS TOUGH GANGSTER ACT. GOD, HOW PREDICTABLE. JUST DON'T START SAYING HOW POWERFUL YOU ARE, SHE THOUGHT.

COWBOY, YOU DON'T KNOW HOW MUCH POWER I HAVE HERE. THIS IS A BIG CITY. NOT A COWPOKE RANCH. YOU WERE PAID FOR THE HORSE--NOW GO AWAY.

SURE, I WAS PAID. BUT GUS NEVER GOT HIS. I'M HERE TO COLLECT. NOW.

THE COWBOY WAS HERE ABOUT A HORSE.

SHE WAS INTRIGUED.

SHE TRIED TO PAY ATTENTION.

I PAY GUS ALREADY. SURE.

YOU GOTTA UNDERSTAND: BUSINESS WORK VERY DIFFERENT HERE, COWBOY.

YOU NOT ON THE RANGE WITH YOUR GUNS AND INDIANS.

HA! HA!

SHE COULDN'T TAKE HER EYES OFF HIM, WHILE FRANZ TALKED AND TALKED. A BULLSHIT ARTIST TO THE BITTER END.

AND THE COWBOY LISTENED. COOL AS A CUCUMBER. WASN'T THAT AN AMERICAN SAYING? SHE'D LIKE TO ASK HIM.

SHE WONDERED IF HE EVER WORE SPURS?

SPURS WITH THAT CHINGA - CHINGA SOUND, LIKE IN THE MOVIES.

DID HE RIDE BULLS?

THE MONEY. NOW.

AND THAT WAS IT. VIOLENCE HUNG IN THE AIR.

THE MOMENT OF TRUTH. THE SHOWDOWN.

AREN'T YOU GOING TO COUNT IT?
WHY? SHOULD I? IF IT AIN'T ALL HERE, I KNOW WHERE TO FIND YOU.

AND **THAT** WAS IT. SHE DIDN'T KNOW WHAT HAD REALLY HAPPENED.
AS IF SHE HAD WALKED IN ON THE FINAL SCENE OF A MOVIE.

SHE WAS CONFUSED, BUT HER FUTURE SEEMED TO BRIGHTEN.

SHE KNEW HER TIME WITH FRANZ WAS OVER.

TAXI

SHE DIDN'T KNOW EXACTLY WHAT TO DO NEXT WITH HER LIFE.

BUT THEN AGAIN...

...SHE'D NEVER BEEN WITH A COWBOY BEFORE.
MY PARTNER IS STEALING THAT HORSE BACK RIGHT NOW... WANT TO COME ALONG?
SURE.
LE CONSULAT
TAXI
536A-1

IT COULD BE FUN...
LE CONSULAT
...FOR A WHILE.
FILLBÄCH BROTHERS 2007

21st Century Noir
A CRIMINAL emission by Ed Brubaker and Sean Phillips

The Lover

I was probably in love with Nelly before I met her...
Met her in person, I mean.

We'd been talking on the net for weeks by that time.

I'd be at work, bored out of my mind, and just start IMing her, and she'd ping me right back...
Laughing at whatever joke I made. Like she knew me.

Long before I even saw a picture of her, I was pretty sure she was the one.

But when she brought me back to her hotel room...

When she squeezed me up inside... in the softest place in the world...
I knew for sure then, yeah... I was in love...

And I knew I'd do anything to make it last.
Just to stay like this, forever...
--ALMOST CAN'T BELIEVE IT...
I MEAN, YOU GO ALL YOUR LIFE, JUST WAITING FOR ONE PERSON TO REALLY SEE YOU, Y'KNOW?
I KNOW... YEAH...

BUT... IT'S COMPLICATED, DAVID...

WHAT? WHAT DO YOU MEAN?

C'MON... I'M NOT EXACTLY YOUNG... AND WE MET ANONYMOUSLY...
...DID YOU REALLY THINK THERE'D BE NO COMPLICATIONS...?

And I swear to God, I didn't even notice her wedding ring until then.

The Wife

Part of me knows, before I even say a word, that David will do it.
The way he looks at me, the passion in his hands and his eyes...
The way his cock stands at attention just at the sight of me...

But I've gone through it so many times in my head, so I just say it all...
HE HITS YOU?!
ON THE GOOD DAYS, YEAH...

I tell him about the time Bart tied me to the bed for two days, to punish me.

About how my own husband forced himself on me. Over and over again.

How he videotaped me sucking him off and threatened to put it on YouTube.

How I'm basically a prisoner in my own home.
AND I ALWAYS THOUGHT I WAS SO STRONG, Y'KNOW?

THAT I'D NEVER BE LIKE MY MOM WAS...
BUT... IT TURNS OUT I DON'T KNOW ANYTHING...

THAT I'M JUST SOME SCARED LITTLE GIRL...

...JESUS... JESUS FUCKING CHRIST...

I don't even have to mention that all the money is in Bart's name.
I'M GONNA FUCKING KILL HIM!

I'M GONNA BASH HIS FUCKING BRAINS IN WITH A FUCKING HAMMER...

WAIT... CALM DOWN, DAVID...

PLEASE...
...WE HAVE TO BE SMART ABOUT THIS...

The Husband

You gotta love the internet, don't you?
Whatever gets you off, you can find it there...

Or put it there and let other people get off on what gets you off.
And I'll freely admit I'm more twisted than most people are...

But everyone's twisted in their own way, I mean, aren't they?

HELLO...?
IS SOMEONE THERE?

GGAHHHH!

The kid gives it a try... but he's got nothing...
KRAKK

But then, I knew he was coming, so I had the ADVANTAGE.

See, me and Nelly... we're twisted together...
BETTER GAG HIM, HON... HE'S A SCREAMER..

She likes to watch their eyes as they fuck her... these kids...
Knowing they're in love with her... with her lies...

I like to watch from the hotel room closet, getting off while they plan my murder...

The best, though, is making them watch us... Watching their hearts break...

...Once they realize what's coming next.
...NELLY... NELLY...

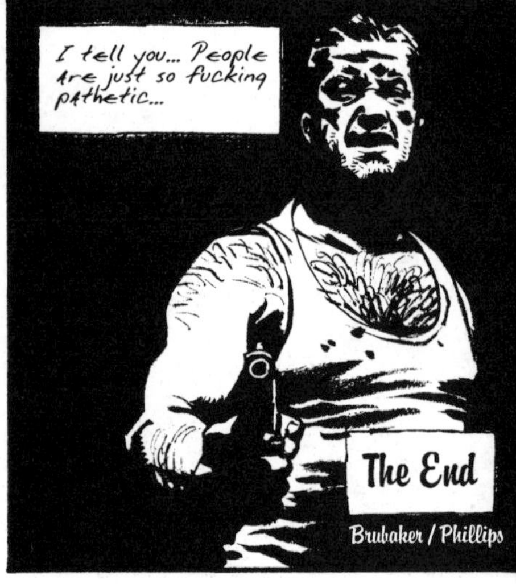
I tell you... People are just so fucking pathetic...
The End
Brubaker / Phillips

MISTER DEWITT?
YES?
I'M SAL'S BROTHER.

WC
SAL'S BROTHER? SIDDOWN.
RUBY!
I'LL HAVE A BEER.
SNIF SNIF
EH-HEM.
SORRY.
YOU GOT A COLD?
SOMETHIN'. I DON' KNOW.
RUBY-- MAKE THAT A VODKA AN' ORANGE JUICE.

YOU GOTTA TAKE CARE OF YERSELF, KID.
BEGGING YER PARDON...
I'M NOT A *KID* NO MORE, SIR.

NO. NO YER NOT.
SO SAL, HE'S TALKED YOU UP.

HE'S MY **BROTHER**. I SUPPOSE THAT'S WHY.
YOU EVER DONE ANY WORK LIKE THIS BEFORE?
BEER
GREEN FALLS BEER

MISTER DEWITT, TIMES BEIN' WHAT THEY ARE..
... I HAVEN'T HAD *ANY* KIND OF WORK IN A WHILE.

THAT *WHY* YER TAKIN' THIS JOB?
CAN I GET ANOTHER?

RUBY!

SAL SAID IT WOULD BE A WALK IN THE PARK.
IT *IS*-- AND THAT'S WHY I'M WILLING TO TRY OUT SAL'S BROTHER.
DO YOU HAVE THE PROPER *TOOLS*?
OKAY.
YOU'LL JUST HAVE TO *SHOW* IT-- NOT USE IT.
BEER
GREEN FALLS BEER
JOB'S AN INSURANCE SCAM. A NECKLACE.
THAT'S *ALL* YER AFTER.
EAT
DRINK
FROM WHO?

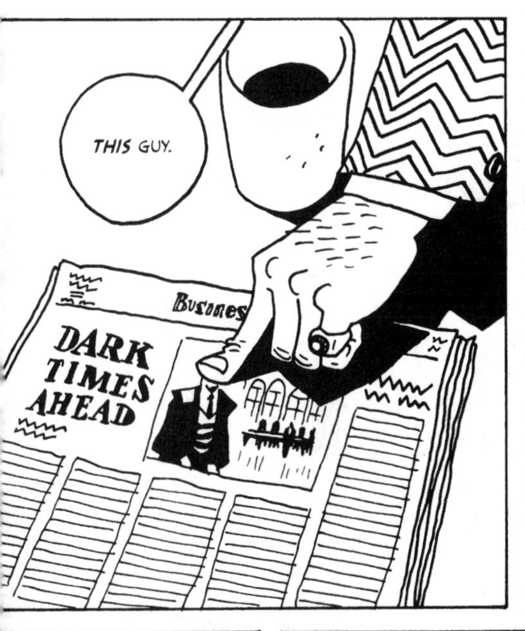
THIS GUY.
Business
DARK TIMES AHEAD

JESUS... YOU GOTTA BE SHITTIN' ME...

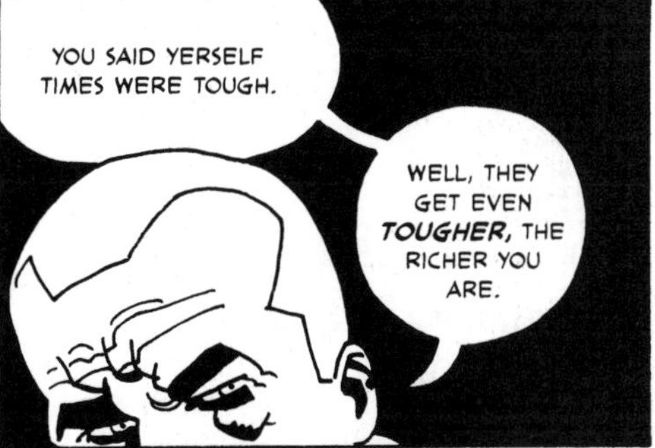
YOU SAID YERSELF TIMES WERE TOUGH.
WELL, THEY GET EVEN TOUGHER, THE RICHER YOU ARE.

RUBY?

WHY DOESN'T HE JUST SELL THE NECKLACE?
WHY DO YOU THINK?

IT MUST BE INSURED FOR MORE THAN IT'S WORTH.

NOW HE-- WHEN YOU DRAW--
HE'S GONNA MAKE A MOVE AT YOU--
TO MAKE IT LOOK GOOD.
WHEN HE DOES-- YOU POP HIM.
WHAT?
WITH THE GUN--
ON THE SIDE OF HIS FUCKIN' HEAD!
SMACK 'IM-- HE'LL GO DOWN. HE AND I--
IT'S PART OF THE SHOW.
RIGHT.
THEN POINT THE GUN AT THE LADY, HAVE HER GIVE YOU THE NECKLACE, AND RUN AWAY.
SAL'LL GET IT FROM YOU TOMORROW.
YOU CAN DO THIS, RIGHT?
I THINK SO.
FUCK YOU THINKING, SAL'S BROTHER.

I'LL GET THE NECKLACE.
GOOD. THAT'S ALL WE WANT.

THEY'RE AT THE PICTURES-- RIGHT NOW. AFTERWARDS, THEY'LL TAKE A WALK-- NOT EXACTLY IN THE PARK-- BUT YOU WILL BE THERE-- WAITING FOR THEM.
ONE MORE THING...

THEY'LL HAVE THEIR KID WITH 'EM.
A KID?

THE BAD NIGHT

AZZARELLO • MOON • BÁ

CREATOR BIOS

BRIAN AZZARELLO is the writer of the multiple award-winning crime epic *100 Bullets* with partner Eduardo Risso, the *New York Times*-bestselling *Joker* with Lee Bermejo, and *Filthy Rich* with Victor Santos, the first book in the Vertigo Crime line. He lives in Chicago with his wife, cartoonist Jill Thompson.

Uruguayan **EDUARDO BARRETO** enjoys international notoriety as the artist behind such titles as *Batman*, *Superman*, *Star Wars*, *Green Arrow*, *Daredevil*, and *Aliens/Predator*. Since 2006, he has been the artist of the long-running *Judge Parker* newspaper strip for King Features.

Since chronicling his youthful life of crime in *Lowlife*, **ED BRUBAKER** has gone on to write many of the top titles at DC and Marvel, winning multiple awards along the way. With artist Sean Phillips, he redefined crime comics in series such as *Sleeper*, *Incognito*, and *Criminal*.

ALEX DE CAMPI is a director and comics writer, best known in comics for the Eisner-nominated political thriller *Smoke*. Her video for the Schema's "Those Rules You Made" was the most popular music video worldwide on YouTube in August 2007.

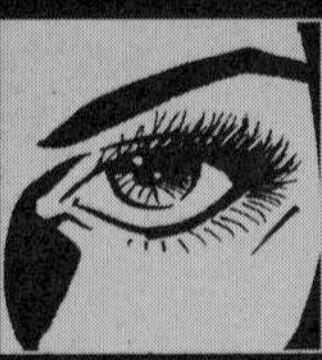

When **MATTHEW** & **SHAWN FILLBÄCH** team up, the results are exciting, off-the-wall, and utterly unique. Their graphic novels include *Road Kill* and *Maxwell Strangewell*, and 2009 saw the launch of *Werewolves on the Moon: Versus Vampires*, written with Dave Land.

Born in Italy, **STEFANO GAUDIANO** moved to America in 1981, where he broke into comics while still in college. In addition to pencilling and inking a variety of comic-book series, he recently opened an Italian-style coffee house in his home of Issaquah, Washington.

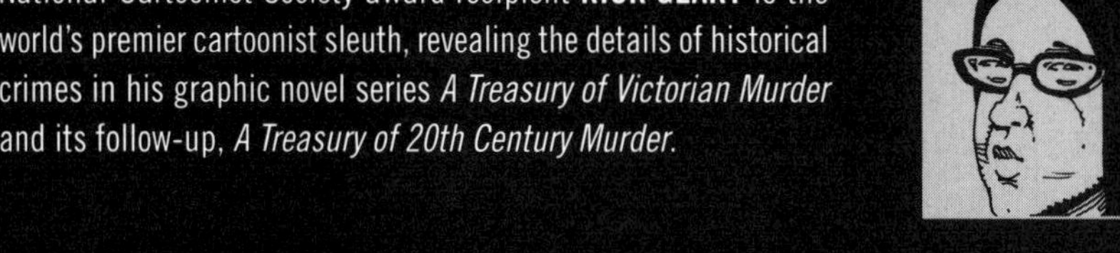

National Cartoonist Society award recipient **RICK GEARY** is the world's premier cartoonist sleuth, revealing the details of historical crimes in his graphic novel series *A Treasury of Victorian Murder* and its follow-up, *A Treasury of 20th Century Murder*.

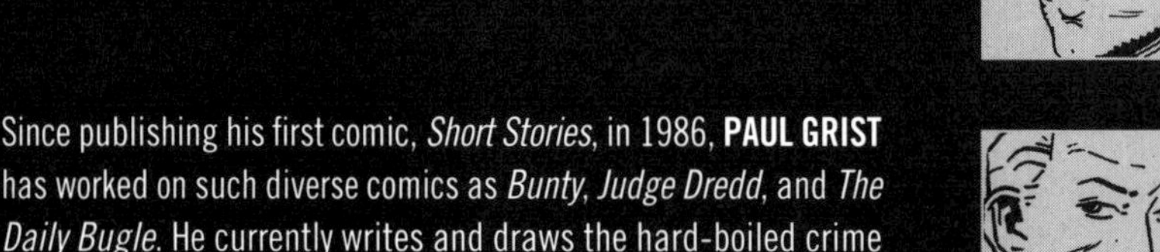

Since publishing his first comic, *Short Stories*, in 1986, **PAUL GRIST** has worked on such diverse comics as *Bunty*, *Judge Dredd*, and *The Daily Bugle*. He currently writes and draws the hard-boiled crime series *Kane* and the offbeat superhero series *Jack Staff*.

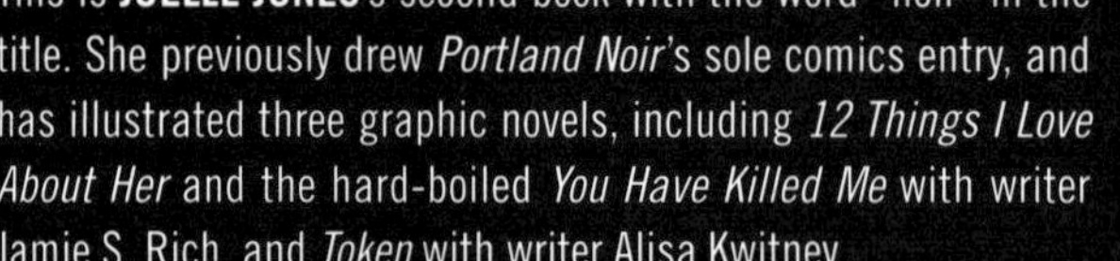

This is **JOËLLE JONES**'s second book with the word "noir" in the title. She previously drew *Portland Noir*'s sole comics entry, and has illustrated three graphic novels, including *12 Things I Love About Her* and the hard-boiled *You Have Killed Me* with writer Jamie S. Rich, and *Token* with writer Alisa Kwitney.

KANO has been drawing comics in Spain and the United States since 1998. In recent years, his dark, moody art has earned him acclaim for blending a crime fiction and pulp sensibility with superheroes in series such as *Gotham Central* and *The Immortal Iron Fist*.

DAVID LAPHAM is best known as the creator of the independent crime series *Stray Bullets*, for which he has won two Eisner awards. Working with DC/Vertigo, he has written and drawn the urban noir graphic novel *Silverfish* and the idiosyncratic series *Young Liars*.

JEFF LEMIRE is the cartoonist behind the Eisner-nominated *Essex County* trilogy of graphic novels published by Top Shelf Productions. His most recent work includes the graphic novel *The Nobody* and the ongoing series *Sweet Tooth*, both from Vertigo.

When shyster **KEN LIZZI** isn't bending the law, he is writing, exercising, brewing beer, traveling, or thinking about traveling. He lives in Portland with his beautiful wife, Isa.

Brazilian twins **FÁBIO MOON** & **GABRIEL BÁ** have been telling stories since 1994. In recent years, working together and separately, they have taken American comics by storm, winning acclaim for both their own work and their collaborations with writers such as Joss Whedon, Gerard Way, and Matt Fraction.

Graphic designer **DEAN MOTTER** revolutionized comics storytelling with *Mister X*. He has gone on to create several more comics stories integrating graphic design and architecture, including *Terminal City* and *Electropolis*, and recently returned to his signature creation with *Mister X: Condemned*.

CHRIS OFFUTT is a writer of short stories, memoirs, novels, and non-fiction, whose work has appeared in anthologies such as *Best American Short Stories* and *New Stories of the South*. Currently he is a producer and writer for Showtime's *Weeds*.

TOM ORZECHOWSKI was the letterer of Marvel's *Uncanny X-Men* for eighteen years, and has been associated with most of the publishers around, including work in manga and in the final true undergrounds. His recent projects include *The Escapists*, *X-Men Forever*, and *Grendel: Behold the Devil*.

Editorial cartoonist and comics artist **M.K. PERKER** is one of his native Turkey's most prominent illustrators, and his American work includes the mystery graphic novel *Insomnia Café*, the Eisner-nominated series *Air* with writer G. Willow Wilson, and illustration for publications such as *The New Yorker*. He lives in New York City.

Spanish graphic designer and advertising artist **HUGO PETRUS** has provided artwork for several entries in the Marvel Illustrated adaptations of classic novels. Most recently, he adapted Jane Austen's *Pride and Prejudice* into comics form with writer Nancy Butler.

GARY PHILLIPS writes tales of mischief and chicanery in various formats. He has a short story in *Phoenix Noir*, and his comics work includes *High Rollers* and *Angeltown*. Like his private eye Ivan Monk, he's weak for donuts and cigars.

In addition to creating *Sleeper*, *Criminal*, and *Incognito* with Ed Brubaker, Eisner Award-winner **SEAN PHILLIPS** has drawn *Marvel Zombies*, *WildC.A.T.s*, *Batman*, and *Hellblazer*. He recently contributed art to the Criterion Collection edition of the 1961 noir film *Blast of Silence*.

Since breaking into comics in 1977, **CLEM ROBINS** has worked with practically everybody, in recent years lettering *100 Bullets*, *Transmetropolitan*, *Preacher*, *Human Target*, and the *Hellboy* line. He has taught human anatomy and figure drawing at the Art Academy of Cincinnati, and is the author of *The Art of Figure Drawing*.